THE BOOK OF EARTH

THE TORCH-BEARERS—II

THE BOOK OF EARTH

BY
ALFRED NOYES

NEW YORK
FREDERICK A. STOKES COMPANY
MCMXXV

CONTENTS

[v]

CONTENTS

CONTENTS

[vii]

I—THE BOOK OF EARTH

I

THE GRAND CANYON

LET the stars fade. Open the Book of
      Earth.

Out of the Painted Desert, in broad noon,
Walking through pine-clad bluffs, in an air
      like wine,
I came to the dreadful brink.

I saw, with a swimming brain, the solid earth
Splitting apart, into two hemispheres,
Cleft, as though by the axe of an angry god.
On the brink of the Grand Canyon,
Over that reeling gulf of amethyst shadows,
From the edge of one sundered hemisphere I
      looked down,
Down from abyss to abyss,

THE TORCH-BEARERS

Into the dreadful heart of the old earth
    dreaming
Like a slaked furnace of her far beginnings,
The inhuman ages, alien as the moon,
Æons unborn, and the unimagined end.
There, on the terrible brink, against the sky,
I saw a black speck on a boulder jutting
Over a hundred forests that dropped and
    dropped
Down to a tangle of red precipitous gorges
That dropped again and dropped, endlessly
    down.

A mile away, or ten, on its jutting rock,
The black speck moved. In that dry diamond
    light
It seemed so near me that my hand could
    touch it.
It stirred like a midge, cleaning its wings in
    the sun.
All measure was lost. It broke—into five
    black dots.
I looked, through the glass, and saw that these
    were men.

[2]

Beyond them, round them, under them, swam
    the abyss
Endlessly on.
          Far down, as a cloud sailed over,
A sun-shaft struck, between forests and sand-
    stone cliffs,
Down, endlessly down, to the naked and
    dusky granite,
Crystalline granite that still seemed to glow
With smouldering colours of those buried
    fires
Which formed it, long ago, in earth's deep
    womb.
And there, so far below that not a sound,
Even in that desert air, rose from its bed,
I saw the thin green thread of the Colorado,
The dragon of rivers, dwarfed to a vein of
    jade,
The Colorado that, out of the Rocky Moun-
    tains,
For fifteen hundred miles of glory and
    thunder,
Rolls to the broad Pacific.
                From Flaming Gorge,

[3]

Through the Grand Canyon with its mon-
strous chain
Of subject canyons, the green river flows,
Linking them all together in one vast gulch,
But christening it, at each earth-cleaving turn,
With names like pictures, for six hundred
miles:
Black Canyon, where it rushes in opal foam;
Red Canyon, where it sleeks to jade again
And slides through quartz, three thousand
feet below;
Split-Mountain Canyon, with its cottonwood
trees;
And, opening out of this, *Whirlpool Ravine,*
Where the wild rapids wash the gleaming
walls
With rainbows, for nine miles of mist and
fire;
Kingfisher Canyon, gorgeous as the plumes
Of its wingèd denizens, glistening with all
hues;
Glen Canyon, where the Cave of Music rang
Long since, with the discoverers' desert-song;
Vermilion Cliffs, like sunset clouds congealed

[4]

To solid crags; the *Valley of Surprise*
Where blind walls open, into a Titan pass;
Labyrinth Canyon, and the *Valley of Echoes;*
Cataract Canyon, rolling boulders down
In floods of emerald thunder; *Gunnison's Valley*
Crossed, once, by the forgotten Spanish Trail;
Then, for a hundred miles, *Desolation Canyon,*
Savagely pinnacled, strange as the lost road
Of Death, cleaving a long deserted world;
Gray Canyon next; then *Marble Canyon,* stained
With iron-rust above, but brightly veined
As Parian, where the wave had sculptured it;
Then deep *Still-water.*

          And all these conjunct
In one huge chasm, were but the towering gates
And dim approaches to the august abyss
That opened here,—one sempiternal page
Baring those awful hieroglyphs of stone,
Seven systems, and seven ages, darkly scrolled

In the deep Book of Earth.

                    Across the gulf
I looked to that vast coast opposed, whose crests
Of raw rough amethyst, over the Canyon, flamed,
A league away, or ten. No eye could tell.
All measure was lost. The tallest pine was a feather
Under my feet, in that ocean of violet gloom.
Then, with a dizzying brain, I saw below me,
A little way out, a tiny shape, like a gnat
Flying and spinning,—now like a gilded grain
Of dust in a shaft of light, now sharp and black
Over a blood-red sandstone precipice.

                          "Look!"
The Indian guide thrust out a lean dark hand
That hid a hundred forests, and pointed to it,
Muttering low, "Big Eagle!"

                       All that day,
Riding along the brink, we found no end.
Still, on the right, the pageant of the Abyss

THE BOOK OF EARTH

Unfolded. There gigantic walls of rock,
Sheer as the world's end, seemed to float in air
Over the hollow of space, and change their
    forms
Like soft blue wood-smoke, with each change
    of light.
Here massed red boulders, over the Angel
    Trail
Darkened to thunder, or like a sunset burned.
Here, while the mind reeled from the im-
    agined plunge,
Tall amethystine towers, dark Matterhorns,
Rose out of shadowy nothingness to crown
Their mighty heads with morning.
                    Here, wild crags
Black and abrupt, over the swimming dimness
Of coloured mist, and under the moving
    clouds,
Themselves appeared to move, stately and
    slow
As the moon moves, with an invisible pace,
Or darkling planets, quietly onward steal
Through their immense dominion.
                  There, far down,

THE TORCH-BEARERS

A phantom sword, a search-beam of the sun,
Glanced upon purple pyramids, and set
One facet aflame in each, the rest in gloom;
While from their own deep chasms of
    shadow, that seemed
Small inch-wide rings of darkness round
    them, rose
Tabular foothills, mesas, hard and bright,
Bevelled and flat, like gems; or, softly
    bloomed
Like alabaster, stained with lucid wine;
Then slowly changed, under the changing
    clouds,
Where the light sharpened, into monstrous
    tombs
Of trap-rock, hornblende, greenstone and
    basalt.

There,—under isles of pine, washed round
    with mist,
Dark isles that seemed to sail through heaven,
    and cliffs
That towered like Teneriffe,—far, far be-
    low,

THE BOOK OF EARTH

Striving to link those huge dissolving steeps,
Gigantic causeways drowned or swam in
    vain,
Column on column, arch on broken arch,
Groping and winding, like the foundered
    spans
Of lost Atlantis, under the weltering deep.
For, over them, the abysmal tides of air,
Inconstant as the colours of the sea,
From amethyst into wreathing opal flowed,
Ebbed into rose through grey, then melted all
In universal amethyst again.
There, wild cathedrals, with light-splintering
    spires,
Shone like a dream in the Eternal mind
And changed as earth and sea and heaven
    must change.
Over them soared a promontory, black
As night, but in the deepening gulf beyond,
Far down in that vast hollow of violet air,
Winding between the huge Plutonian walls,
The semblance of a ruined city lay.
Dungeons flung wide, and palaces brought
    low,

Altars and temples, wrecked and over-
    thrown,
Gigantic stairs that climbed into the light
And found no hope, and ended in the void:
It burned and darkened, a city of porphyry,
Paved with obsidian, walled with serpentine,
Beautiful, desolate, stricken as by strange
    gods
Who, long ago, from cloudy summits, flung
Boulder on mountainous boulder of blood-
    red marl
Into a gulf so deep that, when they fell,
The soft wine-tinted mists closed over them
Like ocean, and the Indian heard no sound.

II

Night and the Abyss

A LONELY cabin, like an eagle's nest,
Lodged us that night upon the monstrous
    brink,
And roofed us from the burning desert stars;
But, on my couch of hemlock as I lay,
The Book of Earth still opened in my
    dreams.
Below me, only guessed by the slow sound
Of forests, through unfathomable gulfs
Of midnight, vaster, more mysterious now,
Breathed that invisible Presence of deep awe.
Through the wide open window, once, a moth
Beat its dark wings, and flew—out—over
    that,
Brave little fluttering atheist, unaware
Of aught beyond the reach of his antennæ,
Thinking his light quick thoughts; while,
    under him,
God opened His immeasurable Abyss.

THE TORCH-BEARERS

All night I heard the insistent whisper rise:
One page of Earth's abysmal Book lies bare.
Read—in its awful hieroglyphs of stone—
His own deep scripture. Is its music sealed?
Or is the inscrutable secret growing clearer?
Then, like the night-wind, soughing through
    the pines,
Another voice replied, cold with despair:
It opens, and it opens. By what Power?
A silent river, hastening to the sea,
Age after age, through crumbling desert rocks
Clove the dread chasm. Wild snows that had
    their birth
In Ocean-mists, and folded their white wings
Among far mountains, fed that sharp-edged
    stream.
Ask Ocean whence it came. Ask Earth. Ask
    Heaven.
I see the manifold instruments as they move,
Remote or near, with intricate inter-play;
But that which moves them, and determines
    all
Remains in darkness. Man must bow his
    head

THE BOOK OF EARTH

Before the Inscrutable.
                    Then, far off, I heard,
As from a deeper gulf, the antiphonal voice:
It opens, and it opens, and it opens,—
The abyss of Heaven, the rock-leaved Book of
    Earth,
And that Abyss as dreadful and profound
Locked in each atom.
                    Under the high stars,
Man creeps, too infinitesimal to be scanned;
And, over all the worlds that dwindle away
Beyond the uttermost microscopic sight,
He towers—a god.
                    Midway, between the height
That crushes, and the depth that flatters him,
He stands within the little ring of light
He calls his knowledge. Its horizon-line,
The frontier of the dark, was narrow, once;
And he could bear it. But the light is grow-
    ing;
The ring is widening; and, with each
    increase,
The frontiers of the night are widening, too.
They grow and grow. The very blaze of truth

*That drives them back, enlarges the grim
      coasts
Of utter darkness.*

              *Man must bow his head
Before the Inscrutable.*

                  Then, from far within,
The insistent whisper rose:

                    *Man is himself
The key to all he seeks.
He is not exiled from this majesty,
But is himself a part of it. To know
Himself, and read this Book of Earth aright;
Flooding it as his ancient poets, once,
Illumed old legends with their inborn fire,
Were to discover music that out-soars
His plodding thought, and all his fables, too;
A song of truth that deepens, not destroys
The ethereal realm of wonder; and still lures
The spirit of man on more adventurous quests
Into the wildest mystery of all,
The miracle of reality, which he shares.*

But O, what art could guide me through that
      maze?

[14]

THE BOOK OF EARTH

What kingly shade unlock the music sealed
In that dread volume?
                         Sons of an earlier age,
Poet and painter stretched no guiding hand.

Even the gaunt spirit, whom the Mantuan led
Through the dark chasms and fiery clefts of
    pain,
Could set a bound to his own realms of
    night,
Enwall then round, build his own stairs to
    heaven,
And slept now, prisoned, in his own coiling
    towers. . . .

Leonardo—found a shell among the hills,
A sea-shell, turned to stone, as at the gaze
Of his own cold Medusa. His dark eyes,
Hawk-swift to hunt the subtle lines of law
Through all the forms of beauty, on that wild
    height
Saw how the waves of a forgotten world
Had washed and sculptured every soaring
    crag,

Ere Italy was born. He stood alone,—
His rose-red cloak out-rippling on the
    breeze,—
A wondering sun-god. Through the moun-
    tain-peaks,
The rumour of a phantom ocean rolled.
It tossed a flying rainbow at his feet
And vanished. . . .

             Milton—walked in Paradise.
He saw the golden compasses of God
Turning through darkness to create the world.
He saw the creatures of a thousand æons
Rise, in six days, out of the mire and clay,
Pawing for freedom. With the great blind
    power
Of his own song, he riveted one more clasp,
Though wrought of fabulous gold, on that
    dark Book,
Not to be loosed for centuries.

                Nearer yet,
Goethe, the torch of science in his own hand,
Poet and seeker, pressed into the dark,
Caught one mysterious gleam from flower and
    leaf,

And one from man's own frame, of that which
    binds
All forms of life together. He turned aside
And lost it, saying, "I wait for light, more
    light."

And these all towered among celestial
    glories,
And wore their legends like prophetic robes;
But who should teach me, in this deeper
    night,
The tale of this despised and wandering
    house,
Our lodge among the stars; the song of
    Earth;
Her birth in a mist of fire,—a ball of flame,
Slowly contracting, crusting, cracking and
    folding
Into deep valleys and mountains that still
    changed
And slowly rose and sank like age-long waves
On the dark ocean of ever-dissolving forms;
Earth, a magical globe, an elfin sphere,
Quietly turning through boundlessness,

Budding with miracles, burgeoning into life;
A murmuring forest of ferns, where the misty
    sun
Saw wingèd monsters fighting to bring forth
    men;
Earth, and her savage youth, her monstrous
    lusts,
Mastered and curbed, till these, too, pulsed
    into music,
And became for man the fountain of his own
    power;
Earth, on her shining way,
Coloured and warmed by the sun, and quietly
    spinning
Her towns and seas to shadow and light in
    turn;
Earth, by what brooding Power
Endowed at birth with those dread potencies
Which out of her teeming womb at last
    brought forth
Creatures that loved and sinned, laughed,
    wept and prayed,
Died, and returned to the unknown Power
    that made them;

THE BOOK OF EARTH

Earth, and that tale of men, the kings of
    thought,
Who strove to read her secret in the rocks,
And turned, amid wild calumny and wrong,
The lucid sword-like search-beams of the
    mind
On the dark passion that through uncounted
    æons
Crept, fought, and climbed to the celestial
    gates,
Three gates in one, one heavenly gate in
    three,
Whose golden names are Beauty, Goodness,
    Truth.

Then, without sound, like an unspoken
    prayer,
The voice I heard upon the mountain height,
Out of a deeper gulf of midnight rose,
Within me, or without, invoking One
To whom this dust, not of itself, would pray:

Muse of the World, O terrible, beautiful
    Spirit,

Throned in pure light, since all the worlds
    obey
Thy golden law which, even here on earth,
Though followed blindly, leads to thy pure
    realm,
Couldst thou deliver me from this night at
    last,
Teach me the burning syllables of thy tongue
That I, even I, out of the mire and clay,
With face uplifted, and with arms up-
    stretched
To the Eternal Sun of Truth, might raise
My song of adoration, not in vain.
Throned above Time, thou sawest when earth
    was born
In darkness, though none else was there to see;
For there was fury in the dark, and fire,
And power, and that creative pulse of thine,
The throb of music, the deep rhythmic
    throes
Of That which made and binds all worlds in
    one.

     *   *   *   *   *   *   *

*In the beginning, God made heaven and
earth.*

THE BOOK OF EARTH

One sentence burned upon the formless
    dark—
One sentence, and no more, from that high
    realm.

The long-sought consummation of all law,
Through all this manifold universe, might
    shine clear
In those eight words one day; not yet; not
    yet!
They would be larger, then;
Not the glib prelude to a lifeless creed,
But wide as the unbounded realms of thought,
The last great simplification of them all,
The single formula, like an infinite sphere
Enfolding Space and Time, atoms and suns,
With all the wild fantastic hosts of life
And all their generations, through all worlds,
In one pure phrase of music, like a star
Seen in a distant sky.
                I could not reach it.
All night I waited for the word in vain.

    *   *   *   *   *   *   *

III

The Wings

NIGHT greyed, and up the immeasurable
abyss,
Brimmed with a blacker night than ocean
knew,
The dawn-wind, like a host of spirits, flowed,
Chanting those airy melodies which, long
since,
The same wild breath, obeying the same
law,
Taught the first pine-woods in the primal
world.

We are the voices.
Could man only
Spell our tongue,
He might learn
The inscrutable secret
And grow young.

THE BOOK OF EARTH

Young as we are
  Who, on shores
    Unknown to man,
Long, long since,
  In waves and woods
    Our song began.

Ere his footsteps
  Printed earth,
    Wild ferns and grass
Breathed it.   No man
  Heard that whispering
    Spirit pass.

Not one mortal
  Lay and listened.
    There was none
Even to hear
  The sea-wave crumbling
    In the sun.

None to hear
  Our choral pine-woods
    Chanting deep,

[23]

THE TORCH-BEARERS

Even as now
  Our solemn cadence
  Haunts your sleep.

Ear was none
  To heed or hear
    When earth was young.
Even now
  Man understands not
    Our strange tongue.

There   came   a   clearer   rustle   of   nearer
    boughs.
A bird cried, once, a sharp ecstatic cry
As if it saw an angel.
                                    He stood there
Against the window's dusky square of sky,
Carrying the long curled crosier of a fern,
My singer of the woods, my Shadow-of-a-
    Leaf,
The invisible friend with whom I used to
    talk
In childhood, and that none but I could
    see,—

THE BOOK OF EARTH

Shadow-of-a-Leaf, shy whisperer of the songs
That none could capture, and so few could
    hear;
A creature of the misty hills of home,
Quick as the thought that hides in the deep
    heart
When the loud world goes by; vivid to me
As flesh and blood, yet with an elfin strain
That set him free of earth, free to run wild
Through all the ethereal kingdoms of the
    mind,
His dark eyes fey with wonder at the world,
And that profoundest mystery of all,
The miracle of reality; clear, strange eyes,
Deep-sighted, joyous, touched with hidden
    tears.
Often he left me when I was not worthy;
And many a time I locked my heart against
    him,
Only to find him creeping in again
Like memory, or a wild vine through a
    window
When I most needed that still voice of his
Which never yet spoke louder than the breath

[25]

Of conscience in my soul. He would return
Quietly as the rustling of a bough
After the bird has flown; and, through a
    rift
Of evening sky, the shining eyes of a child,
The cold clear ripple of thrushes after rain,
The sound of a mountain-brook, or a
    breaking wave
Would teach my slumbering soul the ways of
    love.
He looked at me, more gently than of late,
And spoke (O, if this world had ears to hear
The sound of falling dew, the power that
    wrote
The Paradiso might recall that voice!)
It is near daybreak. I am faithful still;
And I am here to answer all your need.
The hills are old, but not so old as I;
The blackbird's eyes are young, but not so
    young
As mine that know the wonder of their sight.
Eagles have wings. Mine are too swift to see;
For while I stand and whisper at your side,
Time dwindles to a shadow. . . .

                           Like a mist
The world dissolved around us as he spoke.
I saw him standing dark against the sky.
I heard him, murmuring like a spirit in
     trance,—
Dawn on Crotona, dawn without a cloud. . . .

Then, slowly emerging from that mist of
     dreams,
As at an incantation, a lost world
Arose, and shone before me in the dawn.

II—THE GREEKS

I

PYTHAGORAS

I. THE GOLDEN BROTHERHOOD

DAWN on Crotona, dawn without a
     cloud.

In the still garden that Pythagoras made,
The Temple of the Muses, firm as truth,
Lucid as beauty, the white marriage-song
Made visible, of beauty and truth in one,
Flushed with the deepening East.
                  It was no dream.
The thrush that with his long beak shook and
     beat
The dark striped snail-shell on the marble
     flags
Between the cool white columns told me this.

THE TORCH-BEARERS

The birds among the silvery olives pealed
So many jargoning rivulet-throated bells
That in their golden clashings discord
    drowned,
And one wild harmony closed and crowned
    them all
And yet, as if the spread wings of a hawk
Froze in the sky above them, every note
Died on an instant.

                    Over the sparkling grass
The long dark shadows of ash and pine began
To shrink, as though the rising of the sun
Menaced, not only shadows, but the world.

A frightened bird flew, crying, and scattering
    dew
Blindly away; though, on this dawn of dawns,
Nothing had changed. The Golden Brother-
    hood stole
Up through the drifts of wet rose-laurel
    bloom
As on so many a dawn for many a year,
To make their morning vows.

                  They thronged the porch,

THE BOOK OF EARTH

The lean athletes of truth, trained body and
    mind,
For their immortal trial.   Among them
    towered
Milon, the soldier-wrestler. His brown
    limbs
Moved with the panther's grace, the warrior's
    pride;
Milon, who in the Olympic contests won
Crown after crown, but wore them on
    broad brows
Cut like fine steel for thought; and, in his
    eyes,
Carried the light of those deep distances
That challenge the spirit of man.
                    They entered in;
And, like the very Muses following them,
Theano, and her Golden Sisterhood,
First of that chosen womanhood, by the grace
Of whose heaven-walking souls the race
    ascends,
Passed through the shining porch.
                    It was no dream.
In the bright marble, under the sandalled feet,

And in the glimmering columns as they
    passed,
The reflex of their flowing vestments glowed
White, violet, saffron, like another dawn.

*   *   *   *   *   *   *

Before them, through the temple's fragrant
    gloom,
The Muses, in their dim half-circle, towered;
And, in the midst, over the smouldering
    myrrh,
The form of Hestia.
               In her mighty shadow,
Pythagoras, with a scroll in his right hand,
Arose and spoke.
            "Our work is well-nigh done.
Our enemies are closing round us now.
I have given the sacred scrolls into the
    hands
Of Lysis; and, though all else be destroyed,
If but a Golden Verse or two live on
In other lands, and kindle other souls
To seek the law, our work is not in vain.
If it be death that comes to us, we shall lose

Nothing that could endure. It was not
    chance
That sent us on this pilgrimage through
    time,
But that which lives within us, the desire
Of gods, to know what once was dark in
    heaven.
Gods were not gods who, in eternal bliss,
Had never known this wonder—the deep joy
Of coming home. But we have purchased it,
And now return, enriched with memories
Of mortal love, terrestrial grief and pain,
Into our own lost realm."
                  His dark eyes flashed.
He lifted his proud head as one who heard
Strains of immortal music even now.
He towered among the Muses in the dusk,
And then, as though he, too, were carved in
    stone,
And all their voices breathed through his own
    voice,
"Fear nothing now," he said. "Our foes can
    steal
The burdens we lay down, but nothing more.

[33]

All that we are we keep. They strike at
  shadows
And cannot hurt us. Little as we may know,
We have learned at least to know the abiding
  Power
From these poor masks of clay. This dust,
  this flesh,
All that we see and touch, are shadows of it,
And hourly change and perish. Have we not
  seen
Cities and nations, all that is built of earth,
Fleeting into the darkness, like grey clouds,
And only one thing constant—the great law,
The eternal order of their march to death?
Have we not seen it written upon the hills?
The continents and seas do not endure.
They change their borders. Where the seas
  are now
Mountains will rise; and, where the land was,
  once,
The dark Atlantic ends the world for man.
But all these changes are not wrought by
  chance.
They follow a great order. It may be

THE BOOK OF EARTH

That all things are repeated and reborn;
And, in their mighty periods, men return
And pass through their forgotten lives anew.
It may be; for, at times, the mind recalls—
Or half recalls—the turning of a road,
A statue on a hill, a passing face. . . .
It may be; for our universe is bound
In rhythm; and the setting star will rise.
This many a cunning ballad-singer knows
Who haunts the mind of man with dark
    refrains;
Or those deep poets who foretell in verse
The restoration of the world's great Year.
Time never fails. Not Tanais, or the Nile
Can flow for ever. They spring up and
    perish;
But, after many changes, it may be
These, too, return, with Egypt and her kings."

He paused a moment; then compassion, grief,
Wonder and triumph, like one music, spoke
Farewell to shadows, from his own deep soul
Rapt, in pure vision, above the vanishing
    world:

"The torrents drag the rocks into the sea.
The great sea smiles, and overflows the land.
It hollows out the valleys and returns.
The sea has washed the shining rocks away
And cleft the headland with its golden fields
That once bound Sicily to her mother's
    breast.
Pharos, that was an island, far from shore
When Homer sang, is wedded now and one
With Egypt. The wild height where Sappho
    stood,
The beautiful, white, immortal promontory,
Crowned with Apollo's temple, long ago
The struggling seas have severed from the
    land.
And those fair Grecian cities, Helice
And Buris, wondering fishermen see, far
    down,
With snowy walls and columns all aslant,
Trembling under the unremembering wave.
The waters of Anigris, that were sweet
As love, are bitter as death. There was a time
When Etna did not burn. A time will come
When it will cease to burn; for all things
    change;

And mightier things by far have changed
   than these
In the slow lapse of never-ending time.
I have seen an anchor on the naked hills,
And ocean-shells among the mountain-tops.
Continents, oceans, all things pass away;
But One, One only; for the Eternal Mind
Enfolds all changes, and can never change."

II. DEATH IN THE TEMPLE

NIGHT on Crotona, night without a star.
I heard the mob, outside the Temple, roaring
*Death to Pythagoras! Death to those who
   know!*

Before the flushed white columns, in the glare
Of all those angry torches, Cylon stood
Wickedly smiling. "They have barred the
   doors.
Pythagoras and his forty chosen souls
Are all within. They are trapped, and they
   shall die.
It will be best to whet the people's rage

[37]

THE TORCH-BEARERS

Before we lay the axe, or set the torch
Against the Muses' temple. One wild howl
Of 'sacrilege' may defeat us."—This he called
"Faith in the people."

                  He moistened his dry lips,
And raised his hand. The savage clamouring
    ceased.
One breathless moment, ere he spoke, he
    paused,
Gathering his thoughts. His thin white
    weasel face
Narrowed, his eyes contracted. In their pain
—Pain pitiable, a torment of the mind—
A bitter memory burned, of how he sued
To join that golden brotherhood in vain.
For when the Master saw him, he discerned
A spirit in darkness, violent, empty of
    thought,
But full of shallow vanity, cunning lies,
Intense ambition.

            All now was turned to hate;
Hate the destroyer of men, the wrecker of
    cities,
The last disease of nations; hate, the fire

[38]

That eats away the heart; hate, the lean rat
That gnaws the brain, till even reason glares
Like madness through blind eyes; hate,
      the thin snake
That coils like whip-cord round the victim's
      soul
And strangles it; hate, that slides up through
      his throat,
And with its flat and quivering head usurps
The function of his tongue,—to sting and
      sting,
Till all that poison which is now his life
Is drained, and he lies dead; hate, that still
      lives,
And for the power to strike and sting again,
May yet destroy this world.
                              So Cylon stood,
Quivering a moment, in the fiery glare,
Over the multitude.
                        Then, in his right hand,
He shook a roll of parchment over his head,
Crying, *The Master said it!*
                              At that word,
A snarl, as of a myriad-throated beast,

Broke out again, and deepened into a roar—
*Death to Pythagoras! Death to those who
know!*

Cylon upheld his hand, as if to bless
A stormy sea with calm. The howling died
Into a deadly hush. With twisted lips
He spoke.

    "This is their Scroll, the Sacred Word,
The Secret Doctrine of their Golden Order!
Hear it!"
      Then, interweaving truth with lies,
Till even the truth struck like a venomed dart
Into his hearers' minds, he read aloud
His cunningly chosen fragments.

                At the end,
He tore the scroll, and trampled it underfoot.
"Ye have heard," he said. "Ye are kin to all
   the beasts!
And, when ye die, your souls again inhabit
Bodies of beasts, wild beasts, and beasts of
   burden.
Even yet more loathsome—he that will not
   starve

His flesh, and tame himself and all mankind
To bear this golden yoke shall, after death,
Dwell in the flesh of swine. He that rejects
This wisdom shall, hereafter, seek the light
Through endless years, with toads, asps,
    creeping things.
Thus would they exile all our happier gods!
Away with Bacchus and his feasts of joy!
Back, Aphrodite, to your shameful foam!
Men must be tamed, like beasts.
                   The Master said it!
And wherefore? There are certain lordly
    souls
Who rise above the beasts, and talk with gods.
These are his Golden Brotherhood; these
    must rule!
Ye heard that verse from Homer—whom he
    loves—
Homer, the sycophant, who could call a
    prince
'The shepherd of his people.' What are ye,
Even in this life, then, but their bleating
    flocks?
The Master said it!

[41]

                Homer—his demi-god,
Ye know his kind; ye know whence Homer
    sprang;
An old blind beggarman, singing for his food,
Through every city in Greece"—(This Cylon
    called
Honouring the people)—"already he is out-
    worn,
Forgotten, without a word for this young age;
And great Pythagoras crowns him!
                When they choose
Their Golden Brotherhood, they lay down
    their laws,
Declaring none may rule until he learn,
Prostrate himself in reverence to the dead,
And pass, through golden discipline, to power
Over himself and you; but—mark this well—
Under Pythagoras! Discipline! Ah, that
    path
Is narrow and difficult. Only three hundred
    souls,
Aristocrats of knowledge, have attained
This glory. It is against the people's will
To know, or to acknowledge those that know,

Or let their knowledge lead them for one
    hour.
For see—see how the gods have driven them
    mad,
Even in their knowledge! In their own
    Sacred Scroll,
Pythagoras, who derives you from the beasts,
Affirms that earth, this earth beneath our feet,
Spins like a little planet round the sun!"

A brutal bellowing, as of Asian bulls,
Boomed from a thousand mouths. (This
    Cylon called
The laughter of the people and their gods.)
He raised his hand. It ceased.
               "*This* is their knowledge,
And *this*," he cried, "their charter to obscure
What all men know, the natural face of
    things.
This proves their right to rule us from above.
They meet here nightly. Nightly they con-
    spire
Against your rights, your liberties, and mine.
Was it not they who, when the people rose

[43]

THE TORCH-BEARERS

In Sybaris, housed her noble fugitives here?
'And was it not Pythagoras who refused
To send them back to Sybaris and their
    death?
Was it not this that plunged us into war
With Sybaris; and, when victory crowned our
    arms,
Who but Pythagoras robbed us of its fruits?
We gathered booty, and he called it theft.
We burned their palaces, and he called it hate.
We avenged our sons. He called it butchery,
And said the wild beast wakes again in
    man.
What have we gained, then? Nothing but the
    pride
Of saving those Pythagoras wished to save;
Counting gold dross, and serving his pure
    gods.
The Master said it. What is your judgment,
    then?"

He stretched one hand, appealing to the
    crowd,
And one to the white still Temple.
                    "Death! Death! Death!"

THE BOOK OF EARTH

Under the flaring torches, the long waves
Of tense hot faces opened a thousand mouths,
Little blue pits of shadow that raced along
    them,
And shook the red smoke with one volleying
    roar,—
Death to Pythagoras! Death to those who
    know!

    *   *   *   *   *   *   *

But, in the Temple, through those massive
    walls,
While Cylon spoke, no whisper had been
    heard;
Only, at times, a murmur, when he paused,
As of a ninth wave breaking, far away.

The half-moon of the Muses, crowned with
    calm,
Towered through the dimness. Under their
    giant knees,
In their immortal shadow, those who knew
How little was their knowledge waited death
Proudly, around their Master. Robed in
    white,

[45]

Beautiful as Apollo in old age,
He stood amongst them, laying a gentle hand,
One last caress, upon that dearest head
Bowed there before him, his own daughter's
    hair.
Then, tenderly, the god within him moved
His mortal lips; and, in the darkness there,
He spoke, as though the music of the spheres
Welled from his heart, to ease the hurts of
    death.

"Not tears, belovèd. Give it welcome, rather!
Soon, though they spared us, this blind flesh
    would fail.
They are saving us the weary mile or two
That end a dusty journey. The dull stains
Of travel; the soiled vesture; the sick heart
That hoped at every turning of the road
To see the Perfect City, and hoped in vain,
Shall grieve us now no more. Now, at the
    last,
After a stern novitiate, iron test,
And grinding failures, the great light draws
    near,

And we shall pass together, through the
    Veil."

He bowed his head. It was their hour of
    prayer;
And, from among the Muses in the dark,
A woman's voice, a voice in ecstasy,
As if a wound should bless the sword that
    made it,
Breathed through the night the music of
    their law:

Close not thine eyes in sleep
Till thou hast searched thy memories of the
    day,
    Graved in thy heart the vow thou didst
      not keep,
And called each wandering thought back to
    the way.

    Pray to the gods! Their aid,
Their aid alone can crown thy work aright;
    Teach thee that song whereof all worlds
      were made;
Rend the last veil, and feed thine eyes with
    light.

THE TORCH-BEARERS

Naught shall deceive thee, then.
All creatures of the sea and earth and air,
  The circling stars, the warring tribes of
    men
Shall make one harmony, and thy soul shall
    hear.

  Out of this prison of clay
With lifted face, a mask of struggling fire,
  With arms of flesh and bone stretched up
    to pray,
Dumb, thou shalt hear that Voice of thy
    desire.

  Thou that wast brought so low;
And through those lower lives hast risen
    again,
  Kin to the beasts, with power at last to
    know
Thine own proud banishment and diviner
    pain;

Courage, O conquering soul!
For all the boundless night that whelms thee
*   now,*
*   Though worlds on worlds into that dark-*
*   ness roll,*
The gods abide; and of their race art thou!

There was a thunder of axes at the doors;
A glare as of a furnace; and the cry,
Death to Pythagoras! Death to those who
*   know!*

Then, over the streaming smoke and the wild
    light
That like a stormy sunset sank away
Into a darker night, the deeper mist
Rolled down, and of that death I knew no
    more.

II

ARISTOTLE

I. YOUTH AND THE SEA

THE mists unfolded on a sparkling coast
Washed by a violet sea.

It was no dream.
The clustering irised bubbles in the foam,
The grinding stir as through the shining
  pebbles
The wave ran back; the little drifts of smoke
Where wet black rocks dried grey in the hot
  sun;
The pods of sea-weed, crackling underfoot,
All told me this.

My comrade at my side,
Moved like a shadow. I turned a promon-
  tory,
And like a memory of my own lost youth,
Shining and far, across the gulf I saw

[50]

THE BOOK OF EARTH

Stagira, like a little city of snow,
Under the Thracian hills.
                     Nothing had changed.
I saw the City where that Greek was born
Who ranged all art, all life, and lit a fire
That shines yet, after twice a thousand years;
And strange, but strange as truth, it was to
      hear
No slightest change in that old rhythmic
      sound
Of waves against the shore.
                  Then, at my side,
My soul's companion whispered, all unseen,
'Two thousand years have hidden him from
      the world,
Robed him in grey and bearded him with eld,
Untrue to his warm life. There was a time
When he was young as truth is; and the sun
Browned his young body, danced in his young
      grey eyes;
And look—the time is now.'
               There, as he spoke,
I saw among the rocks on my right hand,
Lying, face downward, over a deep rock-pool,

A youth, so still that, till a herring-gull
    swooped
And sheered away from him with a startled
    cry
And a wild flutter of its brown mottled
    wings,
I had not seen him.

              Quietly we drew near,
As shadows may, unseen.

                 He pored intent
Upon a sea-anemone, like a flower
Opening its disk of blue and crimson rays
Under the lucid water.

              He stretched his hand,
And with a sea-gull's feather, touched its
    heart.
The bright disk shrank, and closed, as though
    a flower
Turned instantly to fruit, ripe, soft, and
    round
As the pursed lips of a sea-god hiding there.
They fastened, sucking, on the quill and
    held it.
Young Aristotle laughed. He rose to his feet.

"Come and see this!" he called.

                              Under the cliff

Nicomachus arose, and drawing his robe

More closely round him, crossed the slippery
    rocks

To join his son.

                 There, side by side, they crouched

Over the limpid pool,—the grey physician

And eager boy.

               "See, how it grips the feather!

And grips the rock, too. Yet it has no roots.

Your sea-flowers turn to animals with mouths.

Take out the quill. Now it turns back again

Into a flower; look—look—what lovely
    colours,

What marvellous artistry.

              This never was formed

By chance. It has an aim beyond this pool.

What does it mean? This unity of design?

This delicate scale of life that seems to ascend

Without a break, through all the forms of
    earth

From plants to men? The sea-sponge that I
    found

Grew like a blind rock-rooted clump of moss
Dilating in water, shrinking in the sun;
I know it for a strange sea-animal now,
Shaped like the brain of a man. Can it be true
That, as the poets fable in their songs
Of Aphrodite, life itself was born
Here, in the sea?"

               Nicomachus looked at him.
"That's a dark riddle, my son. You will not
    hear
An answer in the groves of Academe,
Not even from Plato. When you go to
    Athens
Next year, remember, among the loftiest
    flights
Of their philosophy, that the living truth
Is here on earth if we could only see it.
This, this at least, all true Asclepiads know.
Remember, always, in that battle of words,
The truth that father handed down to son
Through the long line of men that served their
    kind
From Æsculapius, father of us all,
To you his own descendant:—naught avails

THE BOOK OF EARTH

In science, till the light you seize from heaven
Shines through the clear sharp fact beneath
    your feet.
This is the test of both—that, in their wed-
    ding,
The light that was a disembodied dream
Burns through the fact, and makes a lanthorn
    of it,
Transfigures it, confirms it, gives it new
And deeper meanings; and itself, in turn,
Is thereby seen more truly.
                    Use your eyes;
And you, or those that follow you, will
    outsoar
Pythagoras.
              He believed the soul descends
From the pure realm of gods; is clothed with
    clay;
And, struggling upward through a myriad
    forms,
After a myriad lives and deaths, returns
Enriched with all those memories, lord of all
That knowledge, master of all those griefs
    and pains

[55]

As else it could not be, home to the gods,
Itself a god, prepared for the full bliss,
The living consummation of the whole.
Earth must be old, if all these things are
    true.
But take this tale and read it. If it seem
Only a tale, the light in it has turned
Dark facts to lanthorns for me. There are
    tales
More true than any fragment of the truth.

One of his homeless clan (who came to
    me
Dying), his last disciple's wandering son,
Gave me the scroll. I give it now to you,—
The young swift-footed runner with the
    fire.
You'll find strange thoughts; and, woven into
    the close,
His Golden Verses, with a thought more
    strange.

Then, from his breast, the Asclepiad drew a
    scroll,

THE BOOK OF EARTH

Smooth as old ivory, honey-stained by time,
A wand of whispering magic; and the boy
Seized it with brown young hands.

                    His father smiled
And turned away, between the shining pools
To seek Stagira. Under his sandalled feet
The   sea-weeds   crackled.   His   footsteps
    crunched away
Along the beach.

                Upon a sun-warmed rock
The boy outspread the curled papyrus-roll,
Keeping each corner in place with a small
    grey stone.
There, while the white robe drifting down the
    coast
Grew smaller and smaller, till at last it
    seemed
A flake of vanishing foam, he lay full length,
Reading the tale.

             The salt on his brown skin
Dried to a faint white powder in the sun.
Over him, growing bold, the peering gulls
Wheeled closer, as he lay there, tranced and
    still;

[57]

Till, through the tale, the golden verses
    breathed
Like a returning music, rhythmic tones
Changed by new voices, coloured by new
    minds,
Yet speaking still for one time-conquering
    soul,
As on the shore the wandering ripples
    changed
And tossed new spray-drops into the sparkling
    air,
Yet pulsed with the ancient breathing of the
    sea:

  Guard the immortal fire.
Honour the glorious line of the great dead.
  To the new height let all thy soul aspire;
But let those memories be thy wine and bread.

  Quench not in any shrine
The smouldering storax. In no human heart
  Quench what love kindled. Faintly though
    it shine,
Not till it wholly dies the gods depart.

[58]

THE BOOK OF EARTH

Truth has remembering eyes.
The wind-blown throng will clamour at
   Falsehood's gate.
Has Falsehood triumphed?   Let the world
   despise
Thy constant mind.   Stand thou aside, and
   wait.

Write not thy thoughts on snow.
Grave them in rock to front the thundering
   sky.
From Time's proud feast, when it is time
   to go,
Take the dark road; bid one more world
   good-bye.

The lie may steal an hour.
The truth has living roots, and they strike
   deep.
A moment's glory kills the rootless flower,
While the true stem is gathering strength in
   sleep.

THE TORCH-BEARERS

Out of this earth, this dust,
Out of this flesh, this blood, this living tomb;
  Out of these cosmic throes of wrath and
      lust,
Breaks the lost splendour from the world's
  blind womb.

  Courage, O conquering soul!
For all the boundless night that whelms thee
    now,
  Though suns and stars into oblivion roll,
The gods abide, and of their race art thou.

II. THE EXILE

TIME dwindled to a shadow. The grey
    mist,
Wreathed with old legends, drifted slowly
    away
From the clear hill-top, where the invisible
    wings
Had brought me through the years.

                        It was no dream.
Clearly, as in a picture, at my feet,

[60]

THE BOOK OF EARTH

Among dark groves, the columned temples
    gleamed,
And I saw Athens, in the sunset, dying.

Dying; for though her shrines had not yet
    lost
One radiant grain of what lies crumbling now
Like a god's bones upon the naked hills;
Though the whole city wound through gate
    on gate
Of visionary splendour to one height
Where, throned above this world, the
    Parthenon
Smiled at the thought of Time, her violet
    crown
Was woven of shadows from a darker realm,
And I saw Athens, dying.
                From that hill—
The hill of Lycabettus—on our right
Eridanus flowed, Ilissus on the left,
Girdling the City like two coils of fire.
Then, as a spirit sees, I saw, unseen,
One standing near me on the bare hillside,
Still as a statue, gazing to the west;

So still that, till his lengthening shadow crept
Up to my feet, the wonder of the City
Withheld my gaze from something more
  august
In that one lonely presence.
       Earth and sun,
On their great way, revealed him, with the
  touch
Of his long stealing shadow; yet it seemed
The power that cast it was no mortal power.
He towered against the dying gleams below
Like Truth in exile.
      On him, too, at last
The doom had fallen. Clasping his grey robe
More closely round him, Aristotle looked
Long, long, at his proud City. She had lost
More glories in that sunset than she knew;
For, though the sun went down in kingly gold
To westward, on that darkening eastern hill,
The bearer of a more celestial fire
Now looked his last on Athens.
      Changed, how changed,
Was this grey form from that immortal
  youth

THE BOOK OF EARTH

Who read the Golden Verses by the sea.
His brow was furrowed now; and, on his face,
Life, with her sharp-edged tools of joy and
      pain,
Had deeply engraved a legend of her own.

There, as his lengthening shadow had drawn
      my gaze,
He seemed himself a shadow of vaster things,
A still dark portent of those moving worlds
Whose huge events, unseen and far away,
Had led him thither; and, as he once had
      shaped
Their course, now shaped his destiny and
      doom.

He had ranged all art, all science. He had
      shaped
Kingdoms and kings, by virtue of his part
In the one all-shaping Mind. Had he not
      lived,
The world that never knows its noblest
      powers
Had moved, with half mankind, another way.

There, looking backward, through his life, he
    knew
That, though the gods conceal their ways
    from men,
Yet in their great conjunctures there are
    gleams
That show them at their work. Theirs was
    the word,
Twenty years back, when Philip of Macedon
Summoned him, as the uncrowned king of
    thought,
To teach his eaglet how to use his wings.
For, by that thought, and by the disciplined
    power,
The sovran power of judgment, swift to seize
Causes, effects, and laws, and wield the blind
Unreasoning mass, he had wellnigh brought
    to birth
What Plato saw in vision—a State enthroned
Above the flux of time, Hellas at one,
A harmony of cities, each a chord
In an immortal song of Beauty and Truth,
Freedom and Law. His was the moving
    power,

THE BOOK OF EARTH

Not wholly aware, that strove to an end un-
    seen;
And in that power had Alexander reigned.
Autocrator of the Greek hegemony,
He had rolled all Asia back into the night.
Satraps of Persia, the proud kings of Tyre,
Nineveh, Babylon, Egypt, all bowed down;
And Alexander shaped the conquered world,
But Aristotle shaped the conqueror's mind.
He had shaped that mind to ends not all its
    own.
His was the well-thumbed Odyssey that re-
    posed
Under the conqueror's pillow; his the love,
Fragrant with memories of the hills and sea,
That had rebuilt Stagira; his the voice
In the night-watches; his the harnessed
    thoughts
That, like immortal sentries, mounted guard
In the dark gates of that world-quelling mind.
His was the whisper, the dark vanishing hint,
The clue to the riddle of slowly emerging life
That, imaged in Egyptian granite, rose
Before the silent conqueror when he stared

At that strange shape, half human and half
    brute,
The Sphinx, who knew the secret of the
    world
And smiled at him, and all his victories,
Under the desert stars, while the deep night
Silently deepened round him.
                       Far away,
In Athens, towered the bearer of the fire.
His was the secret harmony of law
That, while the squadrons wheeled in ordered
    ranks,
Each finding its full life only in the whole,
Flashed light upon the cosmos; his the quest
That taught the conqueror how to honour
    truth
And led him, while he watered his proud
    steeds
In all the streams from Danube to the Nile,
To send another army through the wilds,
Ten thousand huntsmen, ranging hills and
    woods
At Aristotle's hest, for birds and beasts;
So that the master-intellect might lay hold

THE BOOK OF EARTH

Upon the ladder of life that mounts through
    Time,
From plants to beasts, and up, through man,
    to God.
So all the might of Macedon had been turned
To serve the truth, and to complete his work
At Athens, for the conquering age to come;
When Athens, like the very City of Truth,
Might shine upon all nations, and might
    wear,
On her clear brows, his glory as her own.

Then came a flying rumour through the night.
Earth's overlord, the autocrator, his friend,
Alexander the Great had fallen in Babylon.
A little cup of poison, subtle drops
Of Lethe—in a cup of delicate gold,—
And the world's victor slept, an iron sleep;
The conqueror, stricken in his conquered city,
Cold, in the purple of Babylon, lay dead:
And the slow tread of his armies as they
    passed,
Soldier by soldier, through that chamber of
    death,

To look their last upon his marble face,
Pulsed like a muffled drum across the world.
Had Aristotle's cunning mixed the draught
That murdered tyranny?   Let that whispered
    lie
Estrange the heart of Macedon.

                    There, in Athens,
It was enough, now that his friend lay dead,
To know that, as the body is rent away
From the immortal soul, his greatness now
Had lost its earthly stay.   His mighty mind
Walked like a ghost in Athens.   It was enough
To hint that he had taught his king too well;
Served him too well; and played the spy for
    him;
While, for main charge, since he had greatly
    loved
The mother who had borne him, since he had
    poured
His love out on her tomb, it would suffice
To snarl that rites like these were meant for
    gods
And that this man who had seen behind the
    world

The Mover of all things, the eternal God,
The supreme Good, by these fond rites of
 love,
Too simple and too great, too clear, too deep,
Had robbed the little sophists of their dues
And so blasphemed against their gods of clay.

*   *   *   *   *   *   *

Hurrying footsteps neared.   He turned and
 saw
His young adopted son and Tyrtamus.
"Nicanor!   Theophrastus!—nay, lift up
Your heads.   You cannot bring me bitterer
 news
Than I foresaw.   I must be brought to judg-
 ment.
But on what grounds?"—
                "Dear father of us all——"
The youth, Nicanor, answered, "When the
 crowd
Grins in the very face of those who ask,
Or think, or dream that truth should be their
 guide;
Nay, grins at truth itself, as at a fool
Tricked in his grandsire's rags, a rustic oaf,

[69]

THE TORCH-BEARERS

A blundering country simpleton who gapes
At the great city's reeling dance of lies,
How can the grounds be wanting?"

      "The true grounds,"
His 'Theophrastus' muttered, "we know too
  well.
Eurymedon, and the rest, those gnat-like
  clans,
The sophists' buzzing swarms, desire a
  change.
They hold with Heraclitus—all things
  change."
His irony stung the youth. His grey eyes
  gleamed.
His voice grew harsh with anger. "Ay, all
  things change!
So justice and injustice, right and wrong,
Evil and good, must wear each other's cloaks;
And, in that chaos, when all excellence
And honour are plucked down, and the clear
  truth
Trampled into the dirt, themselves may rise.
Athens is dying."

     "They speak truly enough

Of all that they can know," the Master said.
"Change is the rhythm that draws this world
    along.
They see the change. Its law they cannot
    see.
But man who is mortal in this body of earth
Has also a part, by virtue of his reason,
In an enduring realm. Their prophet knew
And heard what sophists have no souls to
    hear,—
The Harmony that includes the pulse of
    change;
The divine Reason, past the flux of things;
The eternal Logos, ordering the whole
    world."
And, as he spoke, I heard, through his own
    words,
Tones that were now a part of his own mind,
The murmur of that old legend which he read
So long ago, in boyhood, by the sea.
Time never fails. Not Tanais or the Nile
Can flow for ever. All things pass away
But One, One only; for the eternal Mind
Enfolds all changes, and can never change.

[71]

Tyrtamus touched his arm. "Time presses now.
Come with us. All is ready. On the coast,
In a lonely creek, the quiet keel is rocking.
Three trusty sailors wait us, and at dawn
We, too, shall find new life in a new world
With all that could endure. The voyager knows
The blindness of the cities. Each believes
Its narrow wall the boundary of the world;
And when he puts to sea, their buzzing cries
Fade out behind him like a wrangle of bees."—

"If I remain, what then?"—

                    The hill-top shone
In the last rays. Athens was growing dark.
Tyrtamus answered him. "A colder cup
Of hemlock, and the fate of Socrates."
The Master looked at Athens. Far away
He traced the glimmering aisle of olive-trees
Where, for so long, with many a youthful friend

He had walked, and taught, and striven him-
    self to learn.
Southward, below the Acropolis, he could see
The shadowy precincts of the Asclepiads,
Guarding their sacred spring, the natural
    fount,
Loved for his father's memory.
                            Close beside,
The Dionysiac theatre, like a moon
Hewn from the marble of Hymettus,
    gleamed,
A silvery crescent, dying into a cloud.
There, though the shade of Sophocles had
    fled,
Long since, he heard even now in his deep
    soul
The stately chorus on a ghostly stage
Chanting the praise of thought that builds the
    city,
Hoists the strong sail to cross the hoary sea,
Ploughs the unwearied earth, yokes the wild
    steed
And the untamed mountain-bull; thought that
    contrives

Devices that can cure all ills but death:

Of all strong things none is more strong than
*   man;*
Man that has learned to shield himself from
*   cold*
And the sharp rain; and turns his marvellous
*   arts*
Awhile to evil; and yet again, to good;
Man that is made all-glorious with his city
When he obeys the inviolable laws
Of earth and heaven; but when, in subtle
*   pride,*
He makes a friend of wrong, is driven astray
And broken apart, like dust before the wind.

All now, except the heights, had died away
Into the dark. Only the Parthenon raised
A brow like drifted snow against the west.
He watched it, melting into the flood of night
With all those memories.

               Then he turned and said,
"If in a moment's thoughtless greed I grasped
The prize that Athens offers me to-night,

She is not so rich but this might make her
    poor.
Death wears a gentle smile when we grow
    old;
And I could welcome it. But she shall not
    stain
Her hands a second time. Let Athens know
That Aristotle left her, not to save
His last few lingering days of life on earth
But to save Athens.
              I have truly loved her,
Next to the sea-washed town where I was
    born,
Best of all cities built by men on earth.
But there's another Athens, pure and white,
Where Plato walks, a City invisible,
Whereof this Athens is only a dim shadow;
And I shall not be exiled from that City."

The hilltop darkened. The blind mist rolled
    down;
The voices died. I saw and heard no more.

III—MOVING EASTWARD

I

FARABI AND AVICENNA

GREY mists enfolded Europe; and I
    heard
Sounds of bewildered warfare in the gloom.

Yet, like a misty star, one lampad moved
Eastward, beyond the mountains where of old
Prometheus, in whose hand the fire first shone,
Was chained in agony. His undying ghost
Beheld the fire returning on its course
Unquenched, and smiled from his dark crag
    in peace,
Implacable peace, at heaven.
              Eastward, the fire
Followed the road Pythagoras trod, to meet
The great new morning.
            The grey mists dissolved.

THE TORCH-BEARERS

*And was it I—or Shadow-of-a-Leaf—that
saw*
*And heard, and lived through all he showed
me then?*

I saw a desert blazing in the sun,
Tufts of tall palm; and then—that City of
dreams.
As though an age went past me in an hour
I saw the silken Khalifs and their court
Flowing like orient clouds along the streets
Of Bagdad. In great Mahmoun's train I
saw
Nazzam, who from the Stagirite caught his
fire.
Long had he pondered on the Eternal Power
Who, in the dark palm of His timeless hand
Rolls the whole cosmos like one gleaming
pearl.
Had he not made, in one pure timeless
thought,
All things at once, the last things with the
first,
The first life with the last; so that mankind,

THE BOOK OF EARTH

Through all its generations, co-exists
For His eternal eyes? Yet, from our own
Who in the time-sphere move, the Maker
    hides
The full revolving glory, and unfolds
The glimmering miracles of its loveliness
Each at its destined moment, one by one,
In an æonian pageant that returns
For ever to the night whence it began.
Thus Nazzam bowed before the inscrutable
    Power,
Yet found Him in his own time-conquering
    soul.

I saw the hundred scribes of El Mansour
Making their radiant versions from the
    Greek.
I saw Farabi, moving through the throng
Like a gaunt chieftain. His world-ranging
    eyes
Beheld the Cause of causes.
                              In his mind,
Lucid and deep, the reasoning of the Greeks
Flooded the world with new celestial light,

THE TORCH-BEARERS

Golden interpretations that made clear
To mighty shades the thing they strove to say.

He carried on their fire, with five-score books
In Arabic, where the thoughts of Athens,
    fledged
With orient colours, towered to the pure
    realm
Of Plato; but, returning earthward still,
Would wheel around his Aristotle's mind
Like doves around the cote where they were
    born.
Then the dark mists that round the vision
    flowed
Like incense-clouds, dividing scene from
    scene,
Rolled back from a wide prospect, and I saw,
As one that mounts upon an eagle's wing,
A savage range of mountains, peaked with
    snow,
To northward.
        They glowed faintly, for the day
Was ending, and the shadows of the rocks
Were stretched out to the very feet of night.

Yet, far away, to southward, I could see
The swollen Oxus, like a vanishing snake
That slid away in slippery streaks and gleams
Through his grey reed-beds to the setting sun.
Earthward we moved; and, in the tawny
     plain,
Before me, like a lanthorn of dark fire
Bokhara shone, a city of shadowy towers
Crimsoned with sunset. In its turreted walls
I saw eleven gates, and all were closed
Against the onrushing night.
                  Then, at my side,
My soul's companion whispered, "You shall
     see
The Gates of Knowledge opening here anew.
Here Avicenna dwelt in his first youth."

At once, as on the very wings of night,
We entered. In the rustling musky gloom
Of those hot streets, thousands of falcon eyes
Were round us; but our shadows passed un-
     seen
Into the glimmering palace of the Prince
Whom Avicenna, when all others failed,

Restored to life, and claimed for all reward
Freedom to use the Sultan's library,
The pride of El Mansour; a wasted joy
To the new Sultan. Radiances were there
Imprisoned like the innumerable slaves
Of one too wealthy even to know their names;
Beautiful Grecian captives, bought with gold
From tawny traffickers in the Ionian sea.
A shadow, with a shadow at my side,
I saw him reading there, intent and still,
Under a silver lamp; his dusky brow
Wreathed with white silk, a goblet close at
    hand
Brimmed with a subtle wine that could un-
    cloud
The closing eyes of Sleep.

                          Along each wall
Great carven chests of fragrant cedar-wood
Released the imprisoned magic,—radiant
    scrolls,
Inscribed with wisdom's earliest wonder-cry;
Dark lore; the secrets of the Asclepiads;
History wild as legend; legends true
As history, all being shadows of one light;

THE BOOK OF EARTH

Philosophies of earth and heaven; and rhymes
That murmured still of their celestial springs.
He thrust his book aside, as in despair.
Our shadows followed him through the
    swarming streets
Into the glimmering mosque. I saw him
    bowed
Prostrate in prayer for light, light on a page
Of subtle-minded Greek which many a day
Had baffled him, when he sought therein the
    mind
Of his forerunner.
                    I saw him as he rose;
And, as by chance, at the outer gates he
    met
A wandering vendor of old tattered books
Who, for three dirhems, offered him a prize.
He bought it, out of gentle heart, and found
A wonder on every page,—Farabi's work,
Flooding his Greek with light.
                        He could not see
What intricate law had swept it into his hand;
But, having more than knowledge, he re-
    turned

[83]

THE TORCH-BEARERS

Through the dark gates of prayer; and, pour-
    ing out
His alms upon the poor, lifted his heart
In silent thanks to God.

II

Avicenna's Dream

BUT all these books—for him—were living
thoughts,
Clues to the darker Book of Nature's law;
For, when he climbed, a goat-foot boy, in
Spring
Up through the savage Hissar range, he saw
A hundred gorges thundering at his feet
With snow-fed cataracts; torrents whose
fierce flight
Uprooted forests, tore great boulders down,
Ground the huge rocks together; and every
year
Channelled raw gullies and swept old scars
away;
So that the wildered eagle beating up
To seek his last year's eyry, found that all
Was new and strange; and even the tuft of
pines

That used to guide him to his last year's nest
Had vanished from the crags he knew no
    more.

There, pondering on the changes of the world,
Young Avicenna, with a kinglier eye,
Saw in the lapse of ages the great hills
Melting away like waves; and, from the sea,
New lands arising; and the whole dark earth
Dissolving, and reshaping all its realms
Around him, like a dream.
                              Thus of his hills
And of their high snows flowing through his
    thoughts
Was born the tale that afterwards was told
By golden-tongued Kazwini, and wafted
    thence
Through many lands, from Tartary to Pa-
    meer.
For, cross-legged, in the shadow of a palm,
The hawk-eyed teller of tales, in years un-
    born
Holding his wild clan spell-bound, would in-
    tone

[86]

THE BOOK OF EARTH

The deep melodious legend, flowing thus,
As all the world flows, through the eternal
     mind.

I came one day upon an ancient City.
I saw the long white crescent of its wall
Stained with thin peach-blood, blistered by
     the sun.

I saw beyond it, clustering in the sky,
Ethereal throngs of ivory minarets,
Tall slender towers, each crowned with one
     bright pearl.

It was no desert phantom; for it grew
And sharpened as I neared it, till I saw,
Under the slim carved windows in the towers,
The clean-cut shadows, forked and black and
     small
Like clinging swallows.
               In the midst up-swam
The Sultan's palace with its faint blue domes,
The moons of morning.
               Wreaths of frankincense

THE TORCH-BEARERS

Floated around me as I entered in.
A thousand thousand warrior faces thronged
The glimmering streets. Blood-rubies burned
    like stars
In shadowy silks and turbans of all hues.

The markets glowed with costly merchandise.
I saw proud stallions, pacing to and fro
Before the rulers of a hundred kings.
I saw, unrolled beneath the slender feet
Of slave-girls, white as April's breathing
    snow,
Soft prayer-rugs of a subtler drift of bloom
Than flows with sunset over the blue and grey
And opal of the drifting desert sand.

Princes and thieves, philosophers and fools
Jostled together, among hot scents of musk.
Dark eyes were flashing. Blood throbbed
    darker yet.
Lean dusky fingers groped for hilts of jade.
Then, with a roll of drums, through Eastern
    gates,
Out of the dawn, and softer than its clouds,

THE BOOK OF EARTH

Tall camels, long tumultuous caravans,
Like stately ships came slowly stepping in,
Loaded with shining plunder from Cathay.
I turned and asked my neighbour in the
    throng
Who built that city, and how long ago.
He stared at me in wonder. "It is old,
Older than any memory," he replied.
"Nor can our fathers' oldest legend tell
Who built so great a city."

                       I went my way.
And in a thousand ages I returned,
And found not even a stone of that great City,
Not even a shadow of all that lust and pride.
But only an old peasant gathering herbs
Where once it stood, upon the naked plain.

"What wars destroyed it, and how long ago?"
I asked him. Slowly lifting his grey head,
He stared at me in wonder.

                   "This bleak land
Was always thus. Our bread was always
    black
And our wine harsh. It is a bitter wind

That scourges us.   But where these nettles
    grew
Nettles have always grown.   Nothing has
    changed
In mortal memory here."

                "Was there not, once,
A mighty City?" I said, "with shining streets,
Here, on this ground?"   I spoke with bated
    breath.
He shook his head and smiled, the pitying
    smile
That wise men use to poets and to fools.—
"Our fathers never told us of that City.
Doubtless it was a dream."

                    I went my way.
And in a thousand ages I returned;
And, where the plain was, I beheld the
    sea.
The sea-gulls mewed and pounced upon their
    prey.
The brown-legged fishermen crouched upon
    the shore,
Mending their tarry nets.

                I asked how long

That country had been drowned beneath the
    waves.
They mocked at me. "His wits are drowned
    in wine.
Tides ebb and flow, and fishes leap ashore;
But all our harvest, since the first wind blew,
Swam in deep waters. Are not wrecks
    washed up
With coins that none can use, because they
    bear
The blind old images of forgotten kings?
The waves have shaped these cliffs, dug out
    these caves,
Rounded each agate on this battered beach.
How long? Ask earth, ask heaven. Nothing
    has changed.
The sea was always here."—
                  I went my way.

And in a thousand ages I returned.
The sea had vanished. Where the ships had
    sailed
Warm vineyards basked, among the enfolding
    hills.

THE TORCH-BEARERS

I saw, below me, on the winding road,
Two milk-white oxen, under a wooden yoke,
Drawing a waggon, loaded black with grapes.
Beside them walked a slim brown-ankled girl.
I stood beneath a shadowy wayside oak
To watch them. They drew near.

                              It was no dream.
Blood of the grape upon the wrinkled throats
And smoking flanks of the oxen told me this.
I saw the branching veins and satin skin
Twitch at the flickering touch of a fly. I saw
The knobs of brass that sheathed their curling
        horns,
The moist black muzzles.

                      Like many whose coats are white,
Their big dark eyes had mists of blue.

                                    Their breath
Was meadows newly mown.

                                By all the gods
That ever wrung man's heart out in the grave
I did not dream this life into the world.—
Blood of the grape upon the girl's brown arms
And lean, young, bird-like fingers told me
        this.

Her smooth feet powdered by the warm grey
    dust;
The grape-stalk that she held in her white
    teeth;
Her mouth a redder rose than Omar knew;
Her eyes, dark pools where stars could shine
    by day;
These were no dream. And yet,—
                  "How long ago,"
I asked her, "did the bitter sea withdraw
Its foam from all your happy sun-burnt
    hills?"
She looked at me in fear. Then, with a smile,
She answered, "Nothing here has ever
    changed.
My father's father, in his childhood, played
Among these vines. That oak-tree where you
    stand
Had lived a century, then. The parent oak
From which its acorn dropped had long been
    dead.
But hills are hills. I never saw the sea.
Nothing has ever changed."
                  I went my way.

[93]

Last, in a thousand ages I returned,
And found, once more, a City, thronged and
    tall,
More rich, more marvellous even than the
    first;
A City of pride and lust and gold and grime,
A City of clustering domes and stately towers,
And temples where the great new gods might
    dwell.
But, turning to a citizen in the gates,
I asked who built it and how long ago.
He stared at me as wise men stare at fools;
Then, pitying the afflicted, he replied
Gently, as to a child:
                  "The City is old,
Older than all our histories.   Its birth
Is lost among the impenetrable mists
That shroud the most remote antiquity.
None knows, nor can our oldest legends tell
Who built so great a City."
                      I went my way.

IV—THE TORCH IN ITALY

Leonardo Da Vinci

I

HILLS AND THE SEA

THE mists rolled back. I saw the City
    of Flowers
Far down, upon the plain; and, on the slope
Beside us—we were shadows and unseen,—
Giulio, the painter, sketching rocks and trees.
We watched him working, till a pine-cone
    crackled
On the dark ridge beyond us, and we saw,
Descending from the summits like a god,
A deep-eyed stranger with a rose-red cloak
Fluttering against the blue of the distant hills.

He stood awhile, above a raw ravine,
Studying the furrows that the rains had made

Last winter.   Then he searched among the
  rocks
As though for buried gold.

                        As he drew near
Giulio looked up and spoke, and he replied.
Their voices rose upon the mountain air
Like a deep river answering a brook,
While each pursued his work in his own way.

Giulio.

What are you seeking?   Something you have
  lost?

The Stranger.

Something I hope to find.

Giulio.

                  You dropped it here?
Was it of value?   Not your purse, I hope.

The Stranger.

More precious than my purse.

Giulio.

                    Your lady's ring?
A jewel, perhaps?

        The Stranger.

            A jewel of a sort;
But it may take a thousand years to trace it
Back to its rightful owner.

        Giulio (laughing).

                O, you are bitten
By the prevailing fashion. Since the plough
Upturned those broken statues, all the world
Is relic-hunting; but, my friend, you'll find
No Aphrodite here.

   The Stranger (picking up a fossil).

            And yet I think
It was the sea, from which she rose alive,
That shaped these rocks and left these twisted
    shells

[97]

THE TORCH-BEARERS

Locked up, like stone in stone. They must have lived
Once, in the sea.

Giulio.

Ah, now I understand.
You're a philosopher,—one of those who tread
The dusty road to Nowhere, which they call
Science.

The Stranger.

All roads to truth are one to me.

Giulio.

Sir, you deceive yourself. Your road can lead
Only to error. The Adriatic lies
How many miles away? We stand up here
On these unchanging hills; and yet, to fit
Your theory, you would roll the seas above
The peaks of Monte Rosa.

[98]

THE BOOK OF EARTH

The Stranger.

But these shells?
How did they come here?

Giulio.

Obviously enough,
The sea being where it is, it was the Flood
That left them here.

The Stranger.

Then Noah must have dropped them
Out of his Ark. They never crept so far;
And Noah must have dumped his ballast, too,
Among our hills; for all those rippled rocks
Up yonder were composed of blue sea-clay.
I have found sea-weed in them, turned to
    stone,
The claws of crabs, the skeletons of fish.
Think you that, if your Adriatic lay
Where it now lies, its little sidling crabs
Could scuttle through the Deluge to the hills?
Your Deluge must have risen above the tops

[99]

Of all the mountains. If it rose so high,
Then it embraced the globe, and made our
    earth
One smooth blue round of water. When it
    sank
What chasm received those monstrous cata-
    racts?
Or was the sun so hot it sucked them up
And turned them into a mist?

                      Is not that tale
A racial memory, lingering in our blood,
Of realms that now lie buried in the sea,
Or isles that heaved up shining from the deep
In old volcanic throes?

Giulio.

                  I must confess
I always feel a pang, sir, when I see
A man of talent wasting his fine powers
On this blind road.

The Stranger.

            Show me a better way.

Giulio.

The way of Art, sir.

The Stranger.

Yes. That is a road
I have wished that I might travel. But are
   you sure
Our paths are not eventually the same?
Why have you climbed up here? To paint
   the truth,
As you perceive it, in those rocks and trees.
Suppose that, with your skill of hand, you
   saw
The truth more clearly, saw the lines of
   growth,
The bones and structure of the world you
   paint,
And the great rhythm of law that runs
   through all,
Might you not paint them better even than
   now?
Might you not even approach the final cause

[101]

THE TORCH-BEARERS

Of all our art and science,—the pure truth
Which also is pure beauty?

Giulio.

                         Genius leaps
Like lightning to that mark, sir, and can waive
These pains and labours.

The Stranger.

                         O, I have no doubt
That you are right.   I speak with diffidence,
And as a mere spectator; one who likes
To know, and seizes on this happy chance
Of learning what an artist really thinks.

Giulio.

We artists, sir, are not concerned with laws,
Except to break them.   Genius is a law
Unto itself.

The Stranger.

                         And that is why you've made
[102]

Your wood-smoke blue against that shining
    cloud?
Against the darker background of the hill
It is blue in nature also; but it turns
To grey against the sky.

Giulio.

            I am not concerned
With trivial points.

The Stranger.

          But if they point to truth
Beyond themselves, and through that change
    of colour
Reveal its cause, and knit your scheme in
    law;
Nay, as a single point of light will speak
To seamen of the land that they desire,
Transfiguring all the darkness with one spark,
Would this be trivial? Sir, a touch will do
    it.
Lend me your brush a moment. Had you
    drawn

Your rocks here in the foreground, thus and
    thus,
Following the ribbed lines of those beds of
    clay
As the sea laid them, and the fire upheaved
And cracked them, you'll forgive me if I say
That they'd not only indicate the law
Of their creation; but they'd look like rocks
Instead of——

Giulio.

Pray don't hesitate.

The Stranger.

I speak
As a spectator only; but to me—
Sponges or clouds perhaps——

Giulio.

We artists, sir,
Aim at this very effect. To us, the fact
Is nothing. There is a kingdom of the mind,

[104]

Where all things turn to dreams. Nothing is
    true
In that great kingdom; and our subtlest work
Is that which has no basis.

The Stranger.

                     Then I fear
My thoughts are all astray; for I believed
That kingdom to be more substantial far
Than anything we see; and that the road
Into that kingdom is the road of law
Which we discover here,—the Word made
    Flesh.

Giulio.

I do not understand you—quite. I fear
Yours is the popular view—that art requires
Purposes, meanings, even moralities
With which we artists, sir, are not concerned.

The Stranger.

O, no. I merely inquire. I wish to hear
From one who knows. I am a little puzzled.

[105]

THE TORCH-BEARERS

You have dismissed so much—this outer
    world
And all its laws; and now this other, too.
I am no moralist; but I must confess
That, in the greatest Art, I have always found
A certain probity, a certain splendour
Of inner and outer constancy to law.

Giulio.

All genius is capricious. You'll admit
That men who lived like beasts have painted
    well.

The Stranger.

Yes; but not greatly, except when their own
    souls
Have gripped the beast within them by the
    throat,
And risen again to reassert the law.

Giulio.

Art lives by its technique, a fact the herd

Will never understand. A noble soul
Is useless, if it cannot wield a brush.

The Stranger.

May not technique include control and judg-
     ment?
Alone, they are not enough; but, for the
     heights,
More is required, not less. I'd even add
Some factors you despise.

Giulio.

                    Your shells, for instance?
And that mysterious and invisible sea?

The Stranger.

The sea whence Beauty rose.

Giulio.

                    You have an eye
For Beauty, too. You are a lover of art
And you are rich. What opportunities

THE TORCH-BEARERS

You throw away! Was it not you I saw
Yesterday, in the market-place at Florence,
Buying caged birds and tossing them into the
    air?

The Stranger.

It may have been. I like to see them fly.
The structure of the wing,—I think that men
Will fly one day.

Giulio.

                It was not pity, then?

The Stranger.

I'd not exclude it. As I said before,
I would include much.

Giulio.

             You were speaking, sir,
Of Art. There are so few, so very few
Who understand what Art is.

[108]

THE BOOK OF EARTH

The Stranger.

                          Fewer still
Who know the few to choose.

             Giulio.

                    Perhaps you'd care
To see some work of mine. I do not live
In Florence; but I'd like to set your feet
On the right way. We are a little group
Known to the few that know. You'd find our
    works
Far better worth your buying than caged
    birds.
Pray let me know your name, sir.

          The Stranger.

                   Leonardo.

II

AT FLORENCE

I SAW the house at Florence, cool and white
With violet shadows, drowsing in the sun.
The fountain splashed and bubbled in the
　　court.
Beside it, in a space of softened light,
Under a linen awning, ten feet high,
Roofing a half-enclosure, where three walls
Were tinted to a pine-wood's blue-black
　　shade,
I saw a woman seated on a throne,
And Leonardo, with his radiant eyes,
Glancing from his wet canvas to her face.

Her face was filled with music. Music
　　swelled
Above them, from a gallery out of sight;
And as the soft pulsation of the strings
Died into infinite distances, he spoke.

His voice was more than music. It was
    thought
Ebbing and flowing, like a strange dark sea.

"Listen to me; for I have things to say
That I can only tell the world through you.
Were you not just a little afraid of me
At first? You know by popular report
I dabble in Black Arts, and so I would
To keep you here, an hour or two each day,
Until the mystery we have conjured up
Between us—there again, it came and went—
Smiles at the centuries in their masquerade
As you smiled, then, at me.
                  Not mockery—quite—
Not irony either; something we evoked
That seems to have caught the ironist off his
    guard,
And slyly observes the mocker's naked heel.
So we'll defend humanity, you and I,
Against the worst of tyrannies,—the blind
    sneer
Of intellectual pride. The subtle fool
And cunning sham at least shall meet one gaze

More subtle, more secure; not yours or mine,
But Nature's own—that calm, inscrutable
    smile
Whereby each erring atomy is restored
To its true place, taught its true worth at last,
And heaven's divine simplicity renewed.

Not yours or mine, Madonna. Could I trust
To brush and palette or my skill of hand
For this? Oh, no! We need Black Arts, I
    think,
Black Arts and incantations, or you'd grow
Weary of sitting here.

                Last night I made
Five bubbles of glass—you blow them with a
    pipe
Over a flame,—and set them there to dance
Upon the fountain's feathery crest of spray.
Piero thought it waste of time. He jeers
At these mechanical arts of mine. I watched
That dance and learned a little of the machine
We call the world. I left them leaping there
To catch your eyes this morning, and learned
    more.

So one thing leads to another. A device,
Mechanical as the spinning of the stars
In the Arch-Mechanic's Cosmos, woke a
      gleam
Of wonder; and I lay these Black Arts bare
To make you wonder more.
                    Black Arts, Madonna;
For even such trifles may discover depths
Dark as the pit of death; as when I laid
Dice on a drum, and by their trembling
      showed
Where underneath our armoured city walls
The enemy dug his mines.
                    And now—you smile,
To think how wars are won.
                    Catgut and wood
Have served our wizardry. Yes; that's why
      I set
Musicians in the gallery overhead,
To pluck their strings; and, while you
      listened, so
Painted the living spirit that they bound
With their bright spells before me, in your
      face.

[113]

THE TORCH-BEARERS

Black Arts, Madonna, and cold-blooded, too.
O, sheer mechanical, playing upon your mind
And senses, as they too were instruments,
Or colours to be ground and mixed and used
For purposes that were not yours at all,
Until the living Power that uses me
Breathes on this fabric, also made by hands,
The inscrutable face that smiles all arts
    away.

How many tales I have told you sitting here
To make you see, according to my need,
The comedy of the world, its lights and
    shades:
The sensual feast; the mockery of renown;
Youth and his innocent boastings, unaware
How swiftly run the sands; Youth that be-
    lieves
His own bright scorn for others' aching faults
Has crowned him conqueror; Youth so nobly
    sure
That plans are all achievements; quite, quite
    sure
Of his own victory where all others failed;

THE BOOK OF EARTH

Age, with blind eyes, or staring at defeat,
Dishonoured; Age, in honour, with a wreath
Of fading leaves in one old trembling hand,
And at his feet the dark all-gulfing grave;
Envy, the lean and wizened witch behind him,
Riding on death, like his own crooked
    shadow,
Snapping at heaven with one contemptuous
    hand,
As though she hated God; and, on her face,
A mask of fairness; Envy, with those barbs
Of wicked lightning darting from her flesh;
Envy, whose eyes the palm and olive wound;
Whose ears the laurel and myrtle pierce with
    pain;
A fiery serpent eating at her heart;
A quiver on her back with tongues for arrows.
Each of these pictures left its little shadow,
A little memory in your spellbound face,
And so your picture smiles at all of these,
And at one secret never breathed aloud,
Because I think we knew it all too well.

Once only, in a riddle, I made you smile

At our own secret also, when I said
'If liberty be dear to you, Madonna,
Never discover that your painter's face
Is Love's dark prison.'

                      Sailing to the south
From our Cilicia, you and I have seen
Beautiful Cyprus, rising from the wave;
Cyprus, that island where Queen Venus
    reigned.
The blood of men was drawn to that rough
    coast
As tides, on other shores, obey the moon.
Glens of wild dittany, winding through the
    hills
From Paphos, her lost harbour, to the peak
Of old Olympus, where she tamed the gods,
Enticed how many a wanderer,

                         Odorous winds
Welcomed us, ruffling, crumpling the smooth
    brine
Into a sea of violets. We drew near.
We heard the muffled thunder of the surf!
What ships, what fleets, had broken among
    those rocks!

THE BOOK OF EARTH

We saw a dreadful host of shattered hulls,
Great splintered masts, innumerable keels
With naked ribs, like skeletons of whales
All weltering there, half-buried in the
    sand.
The foam rushed through them. On their
    rotted prows
And weed-grown poops the sea-gulls perched
    and screamed;
And all around them with an eerie cry
An icy wind was blowing.
                                    It would seem
Like the Last Judgment, should there ever
    be
A resurrection of the ships we saw
Lying there dead. These things we saw and
    live.
And now your picture smiles at all of these.
The secret still evades me everywhere;
And everywhere I feel it, close at hand.
Do you remember when Vesuvius flamed
And the earth shivered and cracked beneath
    our feet?
Ten villages were engulfed. I wandered out

THE TORCH-BEARERS

Among the smoking fragments of earth's
    crust
To see if, in that breaking-up of things,
Nature herself had now perhaps unsealed
Some of her hidden wonders.
                      On that day,
I found a monstrous cavern in the hills,
A rift so black and terrible that it dazed me.
I stood there, with my back bent to an arch,
My left hand clutching at my knee, my right
Shading contracted eyes. I strained to see
Into that blackness, till the strong desire
To know what marvellous thing might lurk
    within
Conquered my fear. I took a ball of thread
And tied one end to a lightning-blasted tree.
I made myself a torch of resinous pine
And entered, running the thread through my
    left hand,
On, on, into the entrails of the world.

O, not Odysseus, when his halting steps
Crept through that monstrous hollow to the
    dead,

Felt such a fearful loneliness as I;
For there were voices echoing through *his*
    night,
And shadows of lost friends to welcome him;
But my fierce road to knowledge clove its
    way
Into a silence deeper than the grave,
Into a darkness where not even a ghost
Could stretch its hands out, even in farewell.
And all that I could see around me there
Was my own smoking torchlight, walls of
    rock
And awful rifts where other caverns yawned.
And all that I could hear was my own steps
Echoing through endless darkness, on and
    on.

My thread ran out. My torch was burning
    low,
When, through the darkness, I became
    aware
Of something darker, looming up in front;
Solid as rock, and yet more strange and
    wild

Than any shadow. My flesh and blood
    turned cold
Before that awful Presence in the dark.
I left the thread behind me, and crept on;
Held up the guttering torch; and there, O
    there,
I saw it, and I live.

                  A monstrous thing
With jaws that might have crushed a ship,
    and bones
That might upheave a mountain; a Minotaur,
A dreadful god of beasts, now turned to stone,
Like a great smoke-bleared idol. The wild
    light
Smeared it with blood; a thing that once had
    lived;
A thing that once might turn the sea to mist
With its huge flounderings, and would make
    a spoil
For kingdoms with the ships it drove ashore.
The torchlight flared against it, and went out;
And I groped back, in darkness. . . .

                    And you smile.
O, what a marvel of enginery was there!

THE BOOK OF EARTH

What giant thews and sinews once con-
     trolled
The enormous hinges of the rock-bound bones
I saw in my dark cavern. Yet it perished,
And all its monstrous race has perished, too.
Was it all waste? Did it prepare the way
For lordlier races? Even, perhaps, for men?

Only one life to track these wonders home,
So many roads to follow. Never the light
Till all be travelled.
                    We will not despise
Mechanical arts, Madonna, while we use
These marvellous living instruments of ours.
Rather we'll seek to master for ourselves
The Master's own devices. Birds can fly,
And so shall men, when they have learned the
     law
Revealed in every wing. Far off, I have seen
Men flying like eagles over the highest
     clouds;
Men that in ships like long grey swordfish
     glide
Under the sea; men that in distant lands

Will speak to men in Italy; men that bring
The distant near, and bind all worlds in one.
And yet—I shall not see it. I have explored
This human instrument, traced its delicate
    tree
Of nerves, discovering how the life-blood
    flows
Out of the heart, through every branching
    vein;
And how, in age, the thickening arteries close
And the red streams no longer feed this frame,
And the parched body starves at last and dies.

I have built bridges. Armies tread them now.
The rains will come. The torrents will roll
    down
And sweep them headlong to the sea, one day.
I have painted pictures. Let cicalas chirrup
Of their brief immortality. I know
How soon these colours fade.

               And yet, and yet,
I do not think the Master of us all
Would set us in His outer courts at night
As the Magnificent, once, in the flush of wine,

Set Angelo, to flatter an idle whim
And sculpture him a godhead out of snow.

The work's not wasted. In my youth I
    thought
That I was learning how to live, and now
I see that I was learning how to die.
Then comes the crowning wonder. We strip
    off
The scaffolding; for the law is learned at
    last;
And our reality, Parian then, not snow,
Dares the full sun of morning, fronts the gaze
Of its divine Pygmalion; lives and breathes;
And knows, then, why it passed through all
    those pains.

Now—the last touch of all! And, as this face
Begins to breathe against those ancient rocks,
Let music breathe these arts of mine away."

Music awoke. It throbbed like hidden wings
Above them. Then a minstrel's golden voice,
As from a distance, on those wings arose
And poured the Master's passion into song:

THE TORCH-BEARERS

Burn, Phœnix, burn;
* And, in thy burning, take*
All that love taught me, all I strove to learn,
* All that I made, and all I failed to make.*

If it be true
* That from the fire thou rise*
In splendour, as men say dead worlds renew
* Their light from their own embers in the*
*   skies,*

In thy fierce nest
* I'd share that death with thee,*
To make one shining feather on thy breast
* Of all I am, and all I strove to be.*

The worthless bough
* May kindle a rich coal;*
And in our mingling ashes, how wilt thou
* Know mine from thine, ere both reclothe*
*   thy soul?*

Now—as thy wings
* Arise from this proud fire,*
My dust in thy assumption mounts and sings;
* And, being a part of thee, I still aspire.*

[124]

V—IN FRANCE

Jean Guettard

I

THE ROCK OF THE GOOD VIRGIN

WHO knows the name of Jean Guettard
        to-day?
I wrestled with oblivion all night long.
At times a curtain on a lighted stage
Would lift a moment, and fall back again.
Once, in the dark, a sunlit row of vines
Gleamed through grey mists on his invisible
    hill.
The mists rolled down. Then, like a miser,
    Night
Caught the brief glory in her blind cloak
    anew.
At dawn I heard the voice of Shadow-of-a-
    Leaf

[125]

THE TORCH-BEARERS

Breathing a quiet song. It seemed remote
And yet was near, as when the listener's
    heart
Fills a cold shell with its remembered waves.

"When I was young," said Jean Guettard,
   "My comrades and myself would hide
Beneath a tall and shadowy Rock
   In summer, on the mountain-side.
The wind and rain had sculptured it—
   Such tricks the rain and wind will play,—
To likeness of a Mother and Child;
   But wind and rain," said Jean Guettard,
"Have worn the rocks for many a day."

"The peasants in that quiet valley,
   Among their vineyards bending there,
Called it the Rock of the Good Virgin,
   And breathed it many an evening prayer.
When I grew up I left my home
   For dark Auvergne, to seek and know
How all this wondrous world was made;
   And I have learned," said Jean Guettard,
"How rains can beat, and winds can blow."

THE BOOK OF EARTH

"When I came home," said Jean Guettard,
　"Not fifty years had fleeted by.
I looked to see the Form I loved
　With arms outstretched against the sky.
Flesh and blood as a wraith might go.
　This, at least, was enduring stone.
I lifted heart and eyes aglow,
　Over the vines," said Jean Guettard. . . .

"The rain had beaten, the wind had blown,
　The hill was bare as the sky that day.
Mother and Child from the height had gone.
　The wind and rain," said Jean Guettard,
"Had crumbled even the Rock away."

"Shadow-of-a-Leaf," I whispered, for I saw
The crosier of a fern against the grey;
And, as the voice died, he stood dark before
　　me.
"You sang as though you loved him.　Let the
　　mists
Unfold."
　He smiled.　"See, first, that Rock," he said,
"Dividing them."

THE TORCH-BEARERS

At once, through drifting wreaths
I saw a hill emerging, a green hill
Clothed with the dying rainbow of those
tears
The mist had left there. From the rugged
crest
Slowly the last thin veils dissolved away.
I saw the Rock upstanding on the height
So closely, and so near me, that I knew
Its kinship with the rocks of Fontainebleau;
The sandstone whose red grains for many an
age
Had been laid down, under a vanished sea;
A Rock, upthrust from darkness into light,
By buried powers, as power upthrust it now
In the strong soul, with those remembering
hills,
Till, graven by frost and beaten by wind and
rain,
It slowly assumed the semblance of that Form
Of Love, the Mother, holding in her arms
The Child of Earth and Heaven; a shape of
stone;
An image; but it was not made by hands.

THE BOOK OF EARTH

Footsteps drew near.   I heard an eager voice
Naming a flower in Latin.

                       Up they came—
Each with a bunch of wild flowers in his
      hand,—
A lean old man, with snowy wind-blown hair,
Panting a little; and, lightly at his side,
Offering a strong young arm, a sun-burnt boy,
Of eighteen years, with darkly shining eyes.
It was those eyes, deep, scornful, tender, gay,
Dark fires at which all falsehood must con-
      sume,
That told me who they were—the young
      Guettard,
And his old grandsire.

                  Under the Rock they stood.
"Good-bye.   I'll leave you here," the old man
      said.
"We've had good luck.   These are fine speci-
      mens.
The last, perhaps, that we shall find together;
For when you leave your home to-morrow,
      Jean,
I think you are going on a longer journey

Even than you know.   Perhaps, when you are
    famous,
You will not be so proud as I should be,
Were I still living, to recall the days
When even I, the old apothecary,
Could teach you something."

               Jean caught a wrinkled hand,
Held it between his own, and laughed away
That shadow, but old Descurain looked at
    him,
Proudly and sadly.   "It will not rest with
    you,
Or your affection, Jean.   The world will see
    to it.
The world that knows as much of you and me,
As you and I of how that creeper grew
Around your bedroom window."

                   As he spoke,
Along the lower slopes the mists began
To blow away like smoke.   The patch of
    vines
Crept out again; and, far below I saw,
Sparkling with sun, the valley of the Juine,
The shining river, and the small clear town

Étampes, the grey old church, the clustering
    roofs,
The cobbled square, the gardens, wet and
    bright
With blots of colour.

                "I have lived my life
Out of the world, down there," Descurain
    said,
"Compounding simples out of herbs and
    flowers;
Reading my Virgil in the quiet evenings,
Alone, for all those years; and, then, with you.
O fortunatos—Do we ever know
Our happiness till we lose it? You'll remem-
    ber
Those Georgics—the great praise of Science,
    Jean!
And that immortal picture of the bees!
No doubt you have chosen rightly. For
    myself,
I know, at least, where healing dittany grows,
And where earth's beauty hides in its dark
    heart
An anodyne, at last, for all our pain.

And one thing more I have learned, and see
    with awe
On every side, more clearly, that on earth
There's not one stone, one leaf, one creeping
    thing,
No; nor one act or thought, but plays its part
In the universal drama.
                  You'll look back
One day on this lost bee-like life of mine;
And find, perhaps, in its obscurest hour
And lowliest task, the moment when a light
Began to dawn upon a child's dark mind.
The old pestle and mortar, and the shining
    jars,
The smell of the grey bunches of dried herbs,
The little bedroom over the market-square,
The thrifty little house where you were born,
The life that all earth's great ones would
    despise—
All these, perhaps, were needed, as the hand
That led you, first, in childhood to the hills.
You'll see strange links, threads of effect and
    cause,
In complicated patterns, growing clear

And binding all these memories, each to each,
And all in one; how one thing led to another,
My simples to your love of plants and flowers,
And this to your new interest in the haunts
That please them best—the kinds of earth, the
     rocks,
And minerals that determine where they
     grow,
Foster them, or reject them. You'll discover
That all these indirections are not ruled
By chance, but by dark predetermined laws.
You'll grope to find what Power, what
     Thought, what Will,
Determined them; till, after many a year,
At one swift clue, one new-found link, one
     touch,
They are flooded with a new transfiguring
     light,
Deep as the light our kneeling peasants know
When, dumbly, at the ringing of a bell
They adore the sacred elements; a light
That shows all Nature, of which your life is
     part,
Bound to that harmony which alone sets free;

And every grain of dust upon its way
As punctual to its purpose as a star.

This Rock has played its part in many a life.
We know it, for we see it every day.
No angelus ever rang, but some one's eyes
Were lifted to it; and, returning home,
The wanderer strains to see it from the road.
What is it, then? It plays no greater part
Than any grain of dust beneath our feet,
Could we discern it. A dumb block of stone,
A shadow in the mind, a thought of God,
A little fragment of the eternal order,
That postulates the whole.

                        If we could see
The universal Temple in which it stands
We, too, should bow our heads; for if this
    Form
Were shaped by Chance, it was the self-
    same Chance
That gave us love and death. In this the fool
Descries a reason for denying all
To which our peasants kneel. The years to
    come

THE BOOK OF EARTH

(And you will speed them, Jean) will rather
    make
This dust the floor of heaven."
                        The old man laid
His bunch of herbs and flowers below the
    Rock,
Smiled, nodded, and went his way.
                    "Was it by chance,"
Thought Jean Guettard, "that grandad laid
    them so;
Or by design; or by some vaster art
Transcending, yet including, all our thoughts,
And memories, with those flowers and that
    dumb stone,
As chords in its world-music? Why should
    flowers
Laid thus"—he laid his own at the feet of the
    Rock—
"Transfigure it with such beauty that it stood
Blessing him, from its arch of soft blue sky
Above him, like a Figure in a shrine?"

He touched its glistening grains. "I think
    that Ray
[135]

Was right," he murmured. "This was surely
    made
Under the sea; sifted and drifted down
From vanished hills and spread in level beds,
Under deep waters; compressed by the sea's
    weight;
Upheaved again by fire; and now, once more,
Wears down by way of the rain and brook and
    river,
Back to the sea; but all by roads of law."
Then, looking round him furtively, to make
    sure
No one was near, he dropped upon his knees.
The mist closed over him. Rock and hill
    were lost
In greyness once again.

II

MALESHERBES AND THE BLACK MILESTONES

MOMENTS were years,
Till, at the quiet whisper of Shadow-of-a-
        Leaf,
Those veils withdrew, and showed another
        scene.
I saw two dusty travellers, blithely walking
With staffs and knapsacks, on a straight white
        road
Lined with tall sentinel poplars as to await
A king's return; but scarce a bird took heed
Of those two travel-stained wanderers—Jean
        Guettard
And Malesherbes, his old school-friend.
                        Larks might see
Two wingless dots that crept along the road.
The Duke rode by and saw two vagabonds
With keenly searching eyes, as they jogged on

[137]

To Moulins.   Birds and Duke and horse
    could see,
Against the sky, that old square prison-tower,
The tall cathedral, the dark gabled roofs,
Thronging together behind its moated wall;
But not one eye in all that wide green land
Saw what those two could see; and not one
    soul
Espied the pilgrim thought upon its way
To change the world for man.

                The pilgrim thought!
Say rather the swift hunter, tracking down
More subtly than an Indian the dark spoor
Of his gigantic prey.

                  I saw them halt
Where, at the white road's edge, a milestone
    rose
Out of the long grass, like a strange black
    gnome,
A gnome that had been dragged from his dark
    cave
Under the mountains, and now stood there
    dumb,
Striving to speak.   But what?

"There! There! Again!"
Cried Jean Guettard. They stood and stared
    at it,
But not to read as other travellers use
How far themselves must journey.
                    They knelt down
And looked at it, and felt it with their hands.
A farmer passed, and wondered were they
    mad.
For, when they hailed him, and his tongue
    prepared
To talk of that short cut across the fields
Beside the mill-stream, they desired to know
Whence the black milestone came. It was the
    fourth
That they had passed since noon.
                    He grinned at them.
"Black stones?" he said, "you'll find them all
    the way
To Volvic now!"
                "To Volvic," cried Guettard,
"Volcani vicus!"
                They seized their staffs again;
Halted at Moulins, only to break a crust

Of bread and cheese, and drink one bottle of
    wine,
Then hastened on, following the giant trail,
Milestone by milestone, till the scent grew
    hot;
For now they saw, in the wayside cottages,
The black stone under the jasmine's cluster-
    ing stars;
And children, at the half-doors, wondered
    why
Those two strange travellers pushed the leaves
    away
And tapped upon their walls.

                     At last they saw,
Black as a thundercloud anchored to its hill,
Above the golden orchards of Limagne,
The town of Riom. All its walls were
    black.
Its turreted heights with leering gargoyles
    crawled
Above them, like that fortress of old Night
To which Childe Roland came.

                    No slughorn's note
Challenged it, and they set no lance in rest,

But dusty and lame, with strangely burning
    eyes,
Those footpads, quietly as the ancient Word,
Stole into that dark lair and sought their prey.
Surely, they thought, the secret must be
    known
To some that live, eat, sleep, in this grim den.
Have they not guessed what monster lurks be-
    hind
This blackness?
                In the chattering streets they saw
The throng around the fruit-stalls, and the
    priest
Entering the Sainte Chapelle. With eyes of
    stone
The statue of that lover of liberty
The chancellor, L'Hôpital, from his great
    dark throne
Gazed, and saw less than the indifferent spar-
    row
That perched upon his hand. Barefooted
    boys
Ran shouting round the fountain in the
    square.

THE TORCH-BEARERS

It was no dream. Along the cobbled street,
Clattering like ponies in their wooden shoes,
Three girls went by with baskets full of
    apples.
The princely butcher, standing at his door,
Rosily breathing sawdust and fresh blood,
Sleeked his moustache and rolled an amorous
    eye.
It was no dream.   They lived their light-
    winged lives
In this prodigious fabric of black stone,
Slept between walls of lava, drank their wine
In taverns whose black walls had risen in
    fire;
Prayed on the slag of the furnace; roofed
    their tombs
With slabs of that slaked wrath; and saw no
    more
Than any flock of birds that nightly roost
On the still quivering Etna.

                                It was late,
Ere the two travellers found a wise old host
Who knew the quarries where that stone was
    hewn;

Too far for them that night.   His inn could
    lodge them.
A young roast fowl?   Also he had a wine,
The Duc de Berry, once. . . . Enough! they
    supped
And talked.   Gods, how they talked and ques-
    tioned him,—
The strangest guests his inn had ever seen.
They wished to know the shape of all the
    hills
Around those quarries.   "There were many,"
    he said,
"Shaped at the top like this."   He lifted up
An old round-bellied wine-cup.
                        At the word
He wellnigh lost his guests.   They leapt to
    their feet.
They wished to pay their quittance and press
    on
To see those hills.   But, while they raved, the
    fowl
Was laid before them, luscious, fragrant,
    brown.
He pointed, speechless, to the gathering dusk,

And poured their wine, and conquered.

                          "The Bon Dieu

Who made the sensual part of man be
    praised,"

He said to his wife; "for if He had made a
    world

Of pure philosophers, every tavern in France

Might close its shutters, and take down its
    sign."

So Jean Guettard and Malesherbes stayed and
    supped;

And, ere they slept, being restless, they went
    out

And rambled through the sombre streets
    again.

They passed that haunted palace of Auvergne,

Brooding on its wild memories and grim
    birth;

And from the Sainte Chapelle, uplifting all

That monstrous darkness in one lean black
    spire

To heaven, they heard an organ muttering
    low

[144]

THE BOOK OF EARTH

As though the stones once more were stirred
    to life
By the deep soul within. Then, arched and
    tall,
In the sheer blackness of that lava, shone
One rich stained window, where the Mother
    stood,
In gold and blue and crimson, with the Child.
They looked at it as men who see the life
And light of heaven through the Plutonian
    walls
Of this material universe. They heard
The young-voiced choir, in silver-throated
    peals,
Filling the night with ecstasy. They stood
Bareheaded in the dark deserted street,
Outcasts from all that innocence within,
And silent; till the last celestial cry,
Like one great flight of angels, ebbed away.

III

THE SHADOW OF PASCAL

AT daybreak they pressed on. Strange hills
 arose
Clustering before them, hills whose fragrant
 turf,
Softer than velvet, hid what savage hearts!
At noon they saw, beside the road, a gash
Rending the sunlit skin of that green peace;
An old abandoned quarry, half overgrown
With ferns, and masked by boughs.
      They left the road
And looked at it. Volcanic rock! A flood
Of frozen lava!
They marked its glossy blackness, the rough
 cords
And wrinkles where, as the fiery waves con-
 gealed,
It had crept on a little; and strangely there

New beauty, like the smile on truth's hard
    face,
Gleamed on them. Never did bracken and
    hart's tongue ferns
Whisper a tale like those whose dauntless
    roots
Were creviced in that grim rock. They
    tracked it up
Through heather and thyme. They saw what
    human eyes
Had seen for ages, yet had never seen,—
The tall green hill, a great truncated cone,
Robed in wild summer and haunted by the
    bee,
But shaped like grey engravings that they
    knew
Of Etna and Vesuvius.
                   Near its crest
They saw the sunlight on a shepherd's crook,
Bright as a star. A flock of nibbling sheep
Flowed round it like a cloud, a rambling
    cloud
With drifting edges that broke and formed
    again

Before one small black barking speck that
flew
Swift as a bird about a cloud in heaven.
Thyme underfoot, wild honey in the thyme;
But, under the thyme and honey, if eyes could
see,
In every runnel and crevice and slip and
patch,
A powdery rubble of pumice, black and red,
Flakes of cooled lava and stones congealed
from fire.
It was no dream. A butterfly spread its fans
White, veined with green, on a rock of sunlit
slag,
Slag of the seething furnaces below.
They reached the summit; and, under them,
beheld
The hollow cup, the crater, whence that flood
Out of the dreadful molten heart of the earth
Poured in red fury to create Auvergne.
But now, instead of smoke and fire, they saw
Red of the heather in that deep grassy hollow,
And heard, instead of the hissing of the abyss,
The small grey locust, stridulent in the sun.

They came to Clermont. All its dark old
    streets
Were built of lava. By the *Place de Jaude,*
O, strangely in their own swift race for truth,
They met the phantom of an earlier fire!
They found the house where Pascal first be-
    held
The sunlight, through a window in lava-
    stone;
And many a time had passed, a brooding
    child,
With all his deep celestial thoughts to come,
Through that volcanic porch, but never saw
The wonder of the walls wherein he slept.
They saw, through mists, as I through mists
    discerned
Their own strange drama, that scene within
    the scene.
They climbed the very hill that Pascal made
A beacon-height of truth—the Puy de Dôme,
Where Florin Périer, at his bidding, took
His tubes of soft quicksilver; and, at the base,
And, at the summit, tested, proved, and
    weighed

THE TORCH-BEARERS

The pressure of that lovely body of light,
Our globe-engirdling air. On one swift hint,
One flash of truth that Torricelli caught
From Galileo, and Pascal caught in turn,
He weighed that glory.
                            Ever the drama grew.
The vital fire, in yet more intricate ways
(As life itself, enkindling point by point
In the dark formless embryo, grows to
    power),
Coursed on, from mind to mind, each working
    out
Its separate purpose, yet all linked in one.
For those two pilgrims, on the cone-shaped
    hill
That Pascal knew, and yet had never known,
Met his great spirit among the scoriac flakes,
And found themselves, in vision, on that pure
    height
Where all the paths to truth shall one day
    meet.
They met his brooding spirit as they climbed.
They passed the dead man's words from
    mouth to mouth,

With new significance, deeper and more
  strange
Even than they knew. *"We are on fire to ex-*
  plore
The universe, and build our tower of truth
Into the Infinite. Then the firm earth laughs,
Opens, under its cracked walls, an abyss."—
Lavoisier! Malesherbes! Friends of Jean
  Guettard.
Was it only the whisper of Shadow-of-a-Leaf
  that showed me
Gleams of the Terror approaching, a wild
  storm
Of fiercer, hell-hot lava, and that far sound
Of tumbrils. . . . The Republic has no
  need
Of savants!
     This dream went by, with the
  dead man's words.
They reached the highest crest. Before their
  eyes
The hill-scape opened like a mighty vision
That, quietly, has come true.
      They stood there, dumb,

THE TORCH-BEARERS

To see what they foresaw, the invisible
    thought
Grown firm as granite; for, as a man might
    die
In faith, yet wake amazed in his new world,
They saw those chains of dead volcanoes rise,
Cone behind cone, with green truncated
    crowns,
And smokeless craters, on the dazzling blue.
There, in the very sunlit heart of France,
They saw what human eyes had daily seen
Yet never seen till now. They stood and
    gazed,
More lonely in that loneliness of thought
Than wingèd men, alighting on the moon.

Old as the moon's own craters were those
    hills;
And all their wrath had cooled so long ago
That as the explorers on their downward path
Passed by a cup-shaped crater, smooth and
    green,
Three hundred feet in depth and breadth,
    they saw,

Within it, an old shepherd and his flock
Quietly wandering over its gentle slopes
Of short sweet grass, through clumps of saf-
    fron broom.
They asked him by what name that hill was
    known.
He answered, *The Hen's Nest!*
"Hen's Nest," cried Jean Guettard, "the good
    God grant
This fowl be not a phœnix and renew
Its feathers in Auvergne."
                They chuckled aloud,
And left the shepherd wondering, many a day,
What secret knowledge in the stranger's eye
Cast that uncanny light upon the hill,
A moment, and no more; and yet enough
To make him feel, even when the north wind
    blew,
Less at his ease in that green windless cup;
And, once or twice, although he knew not
    why,
He turned, and drove his flock another way.

IV

AT PARIS

"FEW know the name of Jean Guettard to-
     day,"
Said Shadow-of-a-Leaf; for now the mists
     concealed
All that clear vision. "I often visited him,
Between the lights, in after years. He lived
Alone at Paris then, in two lean rooms,
A sad old prisoner, at the Palais Royal;
And many a time, beside a dying fire,
We talked together. I was only a shadow,
A creature flickering on the fire-lit wall;
But, while he bowed his head upon his hands
And gazed into the flame with misted eyes,
I could steal nearer and whisper time away.
And sometimes he would breathe his thoughts
     aloud;
And when at night his faithful servant, Claire,
Stole into the room to lay his frugal meal,

THE BOOK OF EARTH

She'd glance at him with big brown troubled
    eyes
To find him talking to himself alone.

And sometimes when the masters of the hour
Won easy victories in the light world's fash-
    ion,
With fables, easily spun in light quick minds,
He'd leave the Academy thundering its ap-
    plause,
And there, in his bare room, with none to see
But Shadow-of-a-Leaf, he would unfold
    again
—Smiling a little grimly to himself—
Those curious beautiful tinted maps he drew,
The very first that any man had made
To show, beneath the kingdoms made by man,
The truth, that hidden structure, ribbed with
    rock,
And track the vanished ages by the lives
And deaths imprinted there.
               They had made him rich
In nothing but the truth.
             He had mapped the rocks.

"The time is not yet come," he used to say,
"When we can clothe them with a radiant
  Spring
Of happy meanings. I have never made
A theory. That's for happier men to come;
It will be time to answer the great riddle
When we have read the question.

                 Here and there
Already, I note, they use this work of mine
And shuffle the old forerunner out of sight.
No matter. Let the truth live. I shall watch
Its progress, proudly, from the outer dark;
More happily, I believe, thus free from self,
Than if my soul went whoring after fame.
One thing alone I'll claim. It is not good
To let all lies go dancing by on flowers.
This—what's his name?—who claims to be
  the first
To find a dead volcano in Auvergne,
And sees, in that, only an easy road
To glory for himself, shall find, ere long,
One live volcano in old Jean Guettard.
The fool has forced me to it; for he thinks
That I'll claim nothing. I prefer my peace;

THE BOOK OF EARTH

But truth compels me here.   I'll set my heel
On him, at least.   Malesherbes will bear me
    out.
As for the rest—no theory of the earth
Can live without these rock-ribbed facts of
    mine,
The facts that I first mapped, I claim no
    more.
These rocks, these bones, these fossil ferns and
    shells,
Of which the grinning moon-calf makes a jest,
A byword for all dotage and decay,
Shall yet be touched with beauty, and reveal
The secrets of the book of earth to man."

"He made no theory," whispered Shadow-of-
    a-Leaf,
"And yet, I think, he looked on all these
    things
Devoutly; on a sea-shell turned to stone
As on a sacred relic, at whose touch
Time opened like a gate, and let him pass
Out of this mocking and ephemeral world
Through the eternal ages, home to God.

[157]

THE TORCH-BEARERS

And so I watched him, growing old and grey,
In seeking truth; a man with enemies,
Ten enemies for every truth he told;
And friends that still, despite his caustic
tongue,
Loved him for his true heart.

                  Yet even these
Never quite reached it; never quite discerned
That even his gruffest words were but the
pledge
Of his own passionate truth; the harsh pained
cry
For truth, for truth, of one who saw the
throng
Bewildered and astray, the ways of love
Grown tortuous, and the path to heaven
grown dim
Through man's unheed for truth.

                   I saw him greet
Condorcet, at the Academy. "We have lost
Two members. I condole with you, my
friend.
It is their last *éloges* you'll speak to-day!
How will you bury their false theories?

THE BOOK OF EARTH

In irony, or in academic robes?
No matter. There'll be only one or two
Who really know; and I shall not be there
To vex you, from my corner, with one smile.
Lord, what a pack of lies you'll have to tell!
It is the custom. When my turn arrives—
'Twill not be long,—remember, please, I want
Truth, the whole truth, or nothing."

                     I saw one night
A member walking home with him—to thank
    him
For his support that morning. Jean Guet-
    tard
Turned on his threshold, growling like a bear.
"You owe me nothing. I believed my vote
Was right, or else you never should have had
    it.
Pray do not think I liked you."

                     A grim door
Opened and closed like iron in the face
Of his late friend and now indignant foe;
To whom no less, if he had needed it,
Guettard would still have given his own last
    sou.

He came into his lonely room that night,
And sat and stared into the fluttering fire.
I, Shadow-of-a-Leaf, was there; and I could
    see
More in his eyes than even Condorcet
    saw,
Condorcet, who of all his friends remained
Most faithful to the end.
                    But, at the hour
When Claire would lay his supper, a light
    hand tapped
Timidly on his door. He sat upright
And turned with startled eyes.
                    "Enter," he called.
A wide-eyed, pale-faced child came creeping
    in.
"What! Little Claire!" he cried.
"Your mother is not better!"
                    She stood before him,
The fire-light faintly colouring her thin
    face,—
"M'sieur, she is very ill. You are a doctor.
Come, quickly."
         Through the narrow, ill-lighted streets

THE BOOK OF EARTH

Old Jean Guettard went hobbling, a small
    hand
Clutching his own, and two small wooden
    shoes
Clattering beside him, till the child began
To droop. He lifted her gently in his arms
And hobbled on. The thin, white, tear-stained
    face,
Pressing against his old grey-bristled cheek,
Directed him, now to left and now to right.
"O, quick, M'sieur!" Then, into an alley,
    dark
As pitch, they plunged. The third door on
    the right!
Into the small sad house they went, and
    saw
By the faint guttering candle-light—the
    mother,
Shivering and burning on her tattered bed.
Two smaller children knelt on either side
Worn out with fear and weeping.
                     All that night
Guettard, of all true kings of science then,
Obscure, yet first in France and all the world,

Watched, laboured, bathed the brow and
    raised the head,
Moistened the thirsting lips, and knew it
    vain;
Knew, as I knew, that in a hundred years
Knowledge might conquer this; but he must
    fight
A losing battle, and fight it in the dark
No better armed than Galen.

                      He closed her eyes
At dawn. He took the children to his house;
Prayed with them; dried their tears; and,
    while they slept,
Shed tears himself, remembering—a green
    hill,
A Rock against the sky.

He cared for them, as though they were his
    own.
Guettard, the founder of two worlds of
    thought,
Taught them their letters. "None can tell,"
    he said,
"What harvests are enfolded for the world

THE BOOK OF EARTH

In one small grain of this immortal wheat.
But I, who owe so much to little things
In childhood; and have seen, among the rocks,
What vast results may wait upon the path
Of one blind life, under a vanished sea,
Bow down in awe before this human life."

V

THE RETURN

EVER, as he grew older, life became
More sacred to him.

                  "In a thousand years
Man will look back with horror on this world
Where men could babble about the Lamb of
    God,
Then turn and kill for food one living thing
That looks through two great eyes, so like
    their own.
I have had living creatures killed for me;
But I will have no more."

               "Though Nature laughed
His mood to scorn," said Shadow-of-a-Leaf,
    "the day
Will come (I have seen it come a myriad
    times)
When, through one mood like this, Nature
    will climb

[164]

Out of its nature, and make all things new.
Who prophesied cities, when the first blind
    life
Crawled from the sea, to breathe that strange
    bright air,
And conquer its own past?"—
"I have no theory of this wild strange world,"
Said Jean Guettard,
"But, if the God that made it dies with us
Into immortal life. . . ."
"There, there's the meaning," whispered
    Shadow-of-a-Leaf,
"Could we but grasp it. There's the har-
    mony
Of life, and death, and all our mortal pain."
I heard that old man whispering in the dark,
"O, little human life, so lost to sight
Among the eternal ages, I, at least,
Find in this very darkness the one Fact
That bows my soul before you."
                    Once again

The mists began to roll away like smoke.
I saw a patch of vines upon the hill
Above Étampes; and through the mists I saw

Old Jean Guettard, with snowy wind-blown
    hair,
Nearing the shrouded summit. As he
    climbed,
Slowly the last thin veils dissolved away.
He lifted up his eyes to see the Rock.
The hill was bare. His facts were well con-
    firmed.
Sun, wind, and rain, and the sharp chisels of
    frost
Had broken it down. The Rock was on its
    way
In brook and river, with all the drifting hills,
And all his life, to the remembering sea.
He looked around him, furtively. None was
    near.
Down, on his knees,
Among the weather-worn shards of his lost
    youth,
Dropt Jean Guettard.
             The mist closed over him.
The world dissolved away. The vision died,
Leaving me only a voice within the heart,
Far off, yet near, the whisper of Shadow-of-
    a-Leaf.

THE BOOK OF EARTH

The rain had beaten.   The wind had blown.
*   The hill was bare as the sky that day.*
Mother and Child from the height had gone.
*   The wind and rain, said Jean Guettard,*
Had crumbled even the Rock away.

VI—IN SWEDEN

LINNÆUS

IT was his garden that began it all,
  A magical garden for a changeling child.

"The garden has bewitched him!
Carl! Carl! O, Carl! Now where is that
    elfkin hiding?"

It was the voice of Christina, wife of the
    Pastor,
Nils Linnæus, the Man of the Linden-tree.
Youthful and comely, she stood at her door in
    the twilight,
Calling her truant son.
                              Her flaxen hair
Kerchiefed with crisp white wings; her rose-
    coloured apron
And blue-grey gown, like a harebell, yielding
    a glimpse

[169]

Of the shapeliest ankle and snowiest stocking
    in Sweden;
She stood at her door, a picture breathed upon
    air.

She called yet again, and tilted her head to
    listen
As a faint, flushed, wild anemone turning
    aside
From a breeze out of elf-land, teasing her
    delicate petals,
The breeze of the warm, white, green-veined
    wings of her wooer;
And again, a little more troubled at heart, she
    called,
"Supper-time, Carl!"
            But out of the fragrant pinewoods
Darkening round her, only the wood-pigeon
    cooed.
Down by the lake, from the alders, only the
    red-cap
Whistled three notes. Then all grew quiet
    again.

Yet, he was there, she knew, though he did not
    answer.
The lad was at hand, she knew, though she
    could not see him.
Her elf-child, nine years old, was about and
    around her,
A queer little presence, invisible, everywhere,
    nowhere,
Hiding, intensely still. . . .
                 She listened; the leaves
All whispered, "Hush!"
It was just as though Carl had whispered,
"Hush! I am watching.
"Hush! I am thinking.
"Hush! I am listening, too."

She tiptoed through the garden, her fair head
Turning to left and right, with birdlike
    glances,
Peeping round lichened boulders and clumps
    of fern.
She passed by the little garden his father gave
    him,
Elfdom within an elfdom, where he had sown

THE TORCH-BEARERS

Not only flowers that rightly grow in gardens,
The delicate aristocracies of bloom,
But hedgerow waifs and ragamuffin strays
That sprawled across his borders everywhere
And troubled even the queendom of the rose
With swarming insurrections.

                    At last she saw him,
His tousled head a little golden cloud
Among the dark green reeds at the edge of the
    lake,
Bending over the breathless water to watch—
What?

               She tiptoed nearer, until she saw
The spell that bound him. Floating upon the
    lake,
A yard away, a water-lily closed
Its petals, as an elfin cygnet smooths
Its ruffled plumes, composing them for sleep.

He watched it, rapt, intent.
                   She watched her son,
Intent and rapt, with a stirring at her heart,
And beautiful shining wonder in her eyes,
Feeling a mystery near her.

THE BOOK OF EARTH

Shadow-of-a-Leaf
Whispered. The garden died into the dark.
Mother and child had gone—I knew not
   whither.
It seemed as though the dark stream of the
   years
Flowed round me.
Then, as one that walks all night
Lifts up his head in the early light of dawn,
I found myself in a long deserted street
Of little wooden houses, with thatched roofs.
It was Uppsala.
Over the silent town
I heard a skylark quivering, up and up,
As though the very dew from its wild wings
Were shaken to silvery trills of elfin song.
Tirile, tirile, tirile, it arose,
Praising the Giver of one more shining day.

Then, with a clatter of doors and a yodelling
   call
Of young men's voices, the Svartbäcken
   woke;
And down the ringing street the students came

[173]

THE TORCH-BEARERS

In loose blue linen suits, knapsack on back
And sturdy stick in hand, to rouse old Carl
For their long ramble through the blossom-
    ing fields.
I saw them clustering round the Master's
    door.
I heard their jolly song—*Papa Linnæus:*

Linnæus, Papa Linnæus,
  He gave his pipe a rap.
He donned his gown of crimson.
  He donned his green fur-cap.
He walked in a meadow at daybreak
  To see what he might see;
And the linnet cried, "Linnæus!
  O hide! Here comes Linnæus.
Beware of old Linnæus,
  The Man of the Linden-tree."

So beautiful, bright and early
  He brushed away the dews,
He found the wicked wild-flowers
  All courting there in twos;
And buzzing loud for pardon,
  Sir Pandarus, the bee:

"Vincit Amor, Linnæus,
    Linnæus, Papa Linnæus!"
O, ho, quoth old Linnæus,
    The Man of the Linden-tree.

Quoth he, 'Tis my conviction
    These innocents must be wed!
So he murmured a benediction,
    And blessed their fragrant bed;
And the butterflies fanned their blushes
    And the red-cap whistled in glee,
They are married by old Linnæus,
    Linnæus, Papa Linnæus!
Vivat, vivat Linnæus,
    The Man of the Linden-tree.

Vivat Linnæus! And out the old Master
    came,
Jauntily as a throstle-cock in Spring,
His big bright eyes aglow; the fine curved
    beak,
The kindly lips, the broad well-sculptured
    brow,
All looked as though the wisdom that had
    shaped them

THE TORCH-BEARERS

Desired that they should always wear a smile
To teach the world that kindness makes men
    happy.
He shook his head at his uproarious troop,
And chose his officers for the day's campaign:
One, for a marksman, with a fowling-piece,
To bring down bird or beast, if need arose;
One for a bugler, to recall their lines
From echoing valley and hill, when some-
    thing rare
Lay in the Master's hand; one to make notes
Of new discoveries; one for discipline; all
For seeking out the truth, in youth and joy.
To-day they made for Jumkil, miles away
Along the singing river, where that prize
The *Sceptrum Carolinum* used to grow.
And, ever as they went, Linnæus touched
All that they saw with gleams of new delight.
As when the sun first rises over the sea
Myriads of ripples wear a crest of fire;
And over all the hills a myriad flowers
Lift each a cup of dew that burns like wine;
And all these gleams reflect one heavenly
    light;

He changed the world around him; filled the
    woods
With rapture; made each footpath wind away
Into new depths of elfin-land. The ferns
Became its whispering fringe; and every stile
A faerie bridge into a lovelier world.
His magic sunlight touched the adventurous
    plants
That grew on the thatch of wayside cottages,
Crepis and *Bromus,* with the straggling brood
Of flowers he called *tectorum,* dancing there
Above the heads of mortals, like swart gnomes
In rusty red and gold.

                "My Svartbäck Latin,"
Linnæus laughed, "may make the pedants
    writhe;
But I would sooner take three slaps from
    Priscian
Than one from Mother Nature."

                    Ancient books
Had made their pretty pattern of the world.
They had named and labelled all their flowers
    by rote,
Grouping them in a little man-made scheme

[177]

Empty of true significance as the wheel
Of stars that Egypt turned for her dead kings.
His was the very life-stream of the flowers;
And everywhere in Nature he revealed
Their subtle kinships; wedded bloom and
  bloom;
Traced the proud beauty, flaunting in her
  garden,
To gipsy grandsires, camping in a ditch;
Linked the forgotten wanderers to their
  clan;
Grouped many-coloured clans in one great
  tribe;
And gathered scores of scattered tribes again
Into one radiant nation.

                         He revealed
Mysterious clues to changes wild as those
That Ovid sang—the dust that rose to a stem,
The stem that changed to a leaf, the crowning
  leaf
That changed to a fruitful flower; and, under
  all,
Sustaining, moving, binding all in one,
One Power that like a Master-Dramatist,

THE BOOK OF EARTH

Through every act and atom of the world
Advanced the triumph that must crown the
    whole.
Unseen by man—that drama—here on earth
It must be; but could man survey the whole,
As even now, in flashes, he discerns
Its gleaming moments, vanishing sharp-
    etched scenes
Loaded with strange significance, he would
    know,
Like Shadow-of-a-Leaf, that not a cloud can
    sail
Across a summer sky, but plays its part.
There's not a shadow drifting on the hills,
Or stain of colour where the sun goes down,
Or least bright flake upon the hawk-moth's
    wing
But that great drama needs them.
                     The wild thrush,
The falling petal, the bubble upon the brook,
Each has its cue, to sing, to fall, to shine,
And exquisitely responds. The drunken bee
Blundering and stumbling through a world of
    flowers

Has his own tingling entrances, unknown
To man or to himself; and, though he lives
In his own bee-world, following his own law,
He is yet the unweeting shuttle in a loom
That marries rose to rose in other worlds,
And shapes the wonder of Springs he cannot
    see.
O, little bee-like man, thou shalt not raise
Thy hand, or close thine eyes, or sigh in
    sleep;
But, over all thy freedom, there abides
The law of this world-drama.

                      Under the stars,
Between sweet-breathing gardens in the dusk,
I heard the song of the students marching
    home.
I saw their eyes, mad nightingales of joy,
Shining with youth's eternal ecstasy.
I saw them tossing vines entwined with
    flowers
Over girls' necks, and drawing them all
    along;
Flags flying, French horns blowing, kettle-
    drums throbbing,

And Carl Linnæus marching at their head.
Up to the great old barn they marched for
    supper,—
Four rounds of beef and a cask of ripened ale;
And, afterwards, each with his own flower-
    fettered girl,
They'd dance the rest of the summer night
    away.

Greybeards had frowned upon this frolic
    feast;
But Carl Linnæus told them "Youth's a
    flower,
And we're botanic students."
                       Many a time,
In green fur-cap and crimson dressing-gown,
He sat and smoked his pipe and watched them
    there
On winter nights; and when the fiddles played
His Polish dance, Linné would shuffle it too.
But now, to-night—they had tramped too
    many miles.
The old man was tired. He left them at the
    door,

And turned to his own house, as one who
    leaves
Much that he loved behind him.

                    As he went
They cheered their chief—"Vivat, vivat,
    Linnæus!"
And broke into their frolic song again.

I saw him in the shadowy house alone
Entering the room, above whose happy door
The watchword of his youth and his old
    age
Was written in gold—*Innocue vivito.*
Numen adest.

             I saw him writing there
His last great joyous testament, to be read
Only by his own children, as he thought,
After he'd gone; an ecstasy of praise,
As though a bird were singing in his mind,
Praise, praise, to the Giver of life and love
    and death!

God led him with His own Almighty Hand,
And made him grow up like a goodly tree.

[182]

THE BOOK OF EARTH

God filled his heart with such a loving fire
For truth, that truth returned him love for
    love.
God aided him, with all that his own age
Had yet brought forth, to speed him on his
    way.
God set him in a garden, as of old,
And gave him, for his duty and delight,
The task that he loved best in all the world.
God gave him for his help-mate, from his
    youth
Into old age, the wife he most desired.
'And blessed him with her goodness.
                        God revealed
His secrets to him; touched his eyes with
    light
And let him gaze into His Council Hall.
God so determined even his defeats
That they became his greatest victories.
God made his enemies as a wind to fill
His homeward-rushing sails. Wherever he
    went
The Lord was with him, and the Lord upheld
    him.

And yet, O yet, one glory was to come;
One strangest gate into infinitude
Was yet to be swung back and take him home.
I know not how the fields that gave us birth
Draw us with sweetness, never to be forgotten
Back through the dark.

                  I saw him groping out,
As through a mist, into a shadowy garden;
And this was not Uppsala any more,
But the lost garden where his boyhood
    reigned.
The little dwindling path at Journey's End
Ran through the dark, into a path he knew.

Carl! Carl! Carl! Now where is that elf-
    kin hiding!
Down by the lake, from the alders, only the
    red-cap
Whistled three notes. Then all grew quiet
    again.

Carl! O Carl! Her voice, though he could
    not answer,
Called him. He knew she was there, though
    he could not see her.

He stood and listened. The leaves were lis-
    tening, too.

He tiptoed through the garden. His grey
    head
Turning to left and right with birdlike
    glances.
He passed by the little garden his father gave
    him.
He knew its breath in the night.
                      His heart stood still.
She was there. He saw her at last. Her back
    was towards him.
He saw her fair young head, through the
    deepening shadows,
Bending, breathlessly, forward to watch a
    child
At the edge of the lake, who watched a float-
    ing flower.
He watched her, rapt, intent. She watched
    her son,
Intent and rapt.
Tears in his heart, he waited, dark and still,
Feeling a mystery near him.

VII—LAMARCK AND THE REVOLUTION

I

LAMARCK AND BUFFON

WHAT wars are these? Far off, a bugle
  blew.
Out of oblivion rose the vanished world.
I stood in Amiens, in a narrow street
Outside a dark old college. I saw a boy,
A budding Abbé, pallid from his books,
Beaked like a Roman eagle. He stole out
Between grim gates; and stripping off his
  bands,
Hastened away, a distance in his eyes;
As though, through an earthly bugle, he had
  heard
A deeper bugle, summoning to a war
Beyond these wars, with enemies yet unknown.

[187]

THE TORCH-BEARERS

I saw him bargaining for a starveling horse
In Picardy and riding to the North,
Over chalk downs, through fields of poppied
    wheat.
A tattered farm lad, sixteen years of age,
Followed like Sancho at his master's heel:
Up to the flaming battle-front he rode;
Flinging a stubborn "no" at those who'd send
    him
Back to learn war among the raw recruits,
He took his place before the astonished ranks
Of grenadiers, and faced the enemy's fire.
Death swooped upon them, tearing long red
    lanes
Through their massed squadrons. His com-
    mander fell
Beside him. One by one his officers died.
Death placed him in command. The shat-
    tered troops
Of Beaujolais were wavering everywhere.
"Retreat!" the cry began. In smoke and fire,
Lamarck, with fourteen grenadiers, held on.
"This is the post assigned. This post we hold
Till Life or Death relieve us."

THE BOOK OF EARTH

                        Who assigned it?
Who summoned him thither? And when
        peace returned
Was it blind chance that garrisoned Lamarck
Among the radiant gardens of the south,
Dazzled him with their beauty, and then
        slipt
That volume of Chomel into his hand,
Traité des Plantes?
                        Was it blind accident,
Environment—O, mighty word that masks
The innumerable potencies of God,—
When his own comrade, in wild horse-play,
        wrenched
And crippled him in body, and he returned
Discharged to Paris, free to take up arms
In an immortal army? Was it chance
That lodged him there, despite his own de-
        sire,
So high above the streets that all he saw
Out of his window was the drifting clouds
Flowing and changing, drawing his lonely
        mind
In subtle ways to Nature's pageantry,

THE TORCH-BEARERS

And the great golden laws that governed all?

Was it blind chance that drew him out to
    watch
The sunset clouds o'er Mont Valérien,
Where the same power, for the same purpose,
    drew
Jean Jacques Rousseau? Flowers and the
    dying clouds
Drew them together, and mind from mind
    caught fire?

What universal Power through all and each
Was labouring to create when first they met
And talked and wondered, whether the forms
    of life
Through earth's innumerable ages changed?
Were species constant? Let the rose run wild,
How swiftly it returns into the briar!
Transplant the southern wilding to the north
And it will change, to suit the harsher sky.
Nourish it in a garden,—you shall see
The trailer of the hedgerow stand upright,
And every blossom with a threefold crown.

THE BOOK OF EARTH

Buffon, upon his hill-top at Montbard
In his red turret, among his flowers and birds,
Gazing through all his epochs of the world,
Had guessed at a long ancestry for man,
Too long for the upstart kings.
                              He could not prove it;
And the Sorbonne, with *Genesis* in its hand,
Had frowned upon his æons. *In six days*
God made the heaven and earth.
                              He had withdrawn,
Smiling as wise men smile at children's talk;
And when Lamarck had visited him alone,
He smiled again, a little ironically.
"Six epochs of the world may mean six days;
But then, my friend, six days must also mean
Six epochs. Call it compromise, or peace.
They cannot claim the victory.
                              There are some
Think me too—orthodox. O, I know the
    whine
That fools will raise hereafter. Buffon
    quailed;
Why did not Buffon like our noble selves
Wear a vicarious halo of martyrdom?

THE TORCH-BEARERS

Strange—that desire of small sadistic eyes
At ease on the shore to watch a shipwrecked
    man
Drowning. Lucretius praised that barbarous
    pleasure.
Mine is a subtler savagery. I prefer
To watch, from a little hill above their world,
The foes of science, floundering in the waves
Of their new compromise. Every crooked
    flash
Of irony lightening their dark skies to-day
Shows them more wickedly buffeted, in a sea
Of wilder contradictions.

                           I had no proof.
Time was not ripe. The scripture of the rocks
Must first be read more deeply. But the law
Pointed to one conclusion everywhere,
That forms of flesh and bone, in the long lapse
Of time, were plastic as the sculptor's clay,
And born of earlier forms.

                           Under man's eyes,
Had not the forms of bird and beast been
    changed
Into new species? Children of the wolf,

THE BOOK OF EARTH

Greyhound and mastiff, in their several kinds,
Fawned on his children, slept upon his hearth.
The spaniel and the bloodhound owned one
    sire.
Man's own selective artistry had shaped
New flowers, confirmed the morning glory's
    crown,
'And out of the wild briar evoked the rose.
Like a magician, in a few brief years,
He had changed the forms and colours of his
    birds.
He had whistled the wild pigeons from the
    rocks;
'And by his choice, and nature's own deep law,
Evoked the rustling fan-tails that displayed
Their splendours on his cottage roof, or bowed
Like courtiers on his lawn. The pouter
    swelled
'A rainbow breast to please him. Tumblers
    played
Their tricks as for a king. The carrier flew
From the spy's window, or the soldiers' camp,
The schoolboy's cage, the lover's latticed
    heart,

[193]

And bore his messages over turbulent seas
And snow-capt mountains, with a sinewy wing
That raced the falcon, beating stroke for
    stroke."

II

LAMARCK, LAVOISIER, AND NINETY-THREE

So, seizing the pure fire from Buffon's hand,
Lamarck pressed on, flinging all else aside,
To follow all those clues to his own end.
Ten years he spent among the flowers of
    France,
Unravelling, and more truly than Linné,
The natural orders of their tangled clans;
Then, in "six months of unremitting toil,"
As Cuvier subtly sneered, he wrote his book,
The *Flore Française;* compact, as Cuvier
    knew,
And did not care to say, with ten years'
    thought.
But Buffon did not sneer. The great old man,
A king of men, enthroned there at Montbard,
Aided Lamarck as Jove might aid his son.
He sent the book to the king's own printing
    press.

Daubenton wrote his foreword; and Rousseau
Had long prepared the way.

                        "Linné of France,"
The stream of praise through every salon
    flowed.
Une science à la mode, great Cuvier sneered.

Was it blind chance that crushed Lamarck
    again
Back to his lean-ribbed poverty?

                             Buffon died.
Lamarck, who had married in his prosperous
    hour,
Had five young mouths to feed. With ten
    long years
Of toil he had made the great *Jardin du Roi*
Illustrious through the world. As his reward
The ministers of the king now granted him
A keepership at one thousand francs a year;
And, over him, in Buffon's place, they set
The exquisite dilettante, Bernardin
Saint Pierre, a delicate twitcher of silken
    strings.
Lamarck held grimly to the post assigned.

Under that glittering rose-pink world he
    heard
Titanic powers upsurging from the abyss.
Then, in the blood-red dawn of ninety-three,
The bright crust cracked. The furious lava
    rolled
Through Paris, and a thundercloud of doom
Pealed over thrones and peoples. Flash on
    flash,
Blind lightnings of the guillotine replied.
Blind throats around the headsman's basket
    roared.
The slippery cobbles were greased with hu-
    man blood.
The torch was at the gates of the Bastille.
Old towers, old creeds, old wrongs, at a
    Mænad shout,
Went up in smoke and flame. Earth's dynas-
    ties
Rocked to their dark foundations. Tyrants
    died;
But in that madness of the human soul
They did not die alone. Innocence died;
And pity died; and those whose hands upheld

THE TORCH-BEARERS

The torch of knowledge died in the bestial
    storm.
Lavoisier had escaped. They lured him back
Into the Terror's hot red tiger-mouth,
Promising, "Face your trial with these your
    friends,
And all will be set free. If not, they die."
He faced it, and returned. The guillotine
Flashed down on one and all.
                    Let the wide earth,
Still echoing its old wrath against the kings
And priests who exiled, stoned and burned
    and starved
The bearers of the fire, remember well
How the Republic in its red right hand
Held up Lavoisier's head, and told mankind
In mockery, colder than the cynical snarl
Of Nero, "The Republic has no need
Of savants. Let the people's will be done
On earth, and let the headless trunk of Truth
Be trampled down by numbers. Tread in the
    mire
All excellence and all skill. Daub your raw
    wounds

With dirt of the street; elect the sick to health.
It is the people's will, and they shall live.
Nay, crown the eternal Power who rules by
    law
With this red cap of your capricious will,
And ye shall hear His everlasting voice
More clearly than ye heard it when He
    spoke
In stillness, through the souls of lonely men,
On starry heights. Lift up your heads and
    hear
His voice in the whirling multitude's wild-
    beast roar,
Not these men, but Barabbas."
                            Must the mind
Turn back to tyranny, then, and trust anew
To harnessed might? The listening soul still
    heard
A more imperative call. Though Evil wore
A myriad masks and reigned as wickedly
In peoples as in kings, Truth, Truth alone,
Whether upheld by many or by few,
Wore the one absolute crown. Though Pilate
    flung

His murderous jest at Truth—the law re-
mained
That answered his dark question; man's one
clue,
The law that all true seekers after Truth
Hold in their hands; the law, a golden thread
That, loyally followed, leads them to full
light,
Each by his own dark way, till all the world
Is knit together in harmony that sets free.
Bridge-builders of the universe, they fling
Their firm and shining roads from star to star,
From earth to heaven. At his appointed task,
Lamarck held grimly on (as once he gripped
His wavering grenadiers) till Life or Death
Relieved him. But he knew his cause at last.
Jardin du Roi became *Jardin des Plantes;*
And the red tumult surging round his walls
Died to a whisper of leaves.

His mind groped back,
Back through the inconceivable ages now,
To terrible revolutions of the globe,
Huge catastrophic rendings of the hills,
Red floods of lava; cataracts of fire;

THE BOOK OF EARTH

Monstrous upheavals of the nethermost deep;
Whereby as Cuvier painted them, in hues
Of blind disaster, all the hosts of life
In each æonian period, like a swarm
Of ants beneath the wheels of Juggernaut,
Were utterly abolished.

                            Did God create
After each earth-disaster, then, new hosts
Of life to range her mountains and her seas;
New forms, new patterns, fresh from His
        careless Hand,
Yet all so closely akin to those destroyed?
Or did this life-stream, from one fountain-
        head,
Through the long changes of unnumbered
        years
Flow on, unbroken, slowly branching out
Into new beauty, as a river winds
Into new channels? One, singing through the
        hills,
Mirrors the hanging precipice and the pine;
And one through level meadows curves away,
Turns a dark wheel, or foams along a weir,
Then, in a pool of shadow, drowns the moon.

III

An English Interlude: Erasmus Darwin

ALREADY in England, bearing the same fire,
A far companion whom he never knew
Had long been moving on the same dark
    quest,
But through what quiet secluded walks of
    peace.

Out of the mist emerged the little City
Of Lichfield, clustering round its Minster
    Pool
That, like a fragment of the sky on earth,
Reflected its two bridges, gnarled old trees,
Half-timbered walls; a bare-legged child at
    play
Upon its brink; two clouds like floating
    swans,
Two swans like small white clouds; a boy that
    rode

THE BOOK OF EARTH

A big brown cart-horse lazily jingling by;
And the cathedral, like a three-spired crown,
Set on its northern bank.

                Then, from the west,
Above it, walled away from the steep street,
I saw Erasmus Darwin's bluff square house.
Along its front, above the five stone steps
That climbed to its high door, strange vines
    and fronds
Made a green jungle in their dim prison of
    glass.
Behind, its windows overlooked a close
Of rambling mellow roofs, and coldly stared
At the cathedral's three foreshortened spires,
Which seemed to draw together, as though in
    doubt
Of what lay hidden in those bleak staring
    eyes.

There dwelt that eager mind, whom fools de-
    ride
For laced and periwigged verses on his
    flowers;
Forgetting how he strode before his age,

And how his grandson caught from his right
    hand
A fire that lit the world.

                    I saw him there,
In his brown-skirted coat, among his plants,
Pondering the thoughts, at which that
    dreamer sneered,
Who, through a haze of opium, saw a star
Twinkling within the tip of the crescent
    moon.
Dispraise no song for tricks that fancy plays,
Nor for blind gropings after an unknown
    light,
But let no echo of Abora praise for this
The drooping pinion and unseeing eye.
Seek, poet, on thy sacred height, the strength
And glory of that true vision which shall
    grasp,
In clear imagination, earth and heaven,
And from the truly seen ascend in power
To those high realms whereof our heaven and
    earth
Are images and shadows, and their law
Our shining lanthorn and unfailing guide.

There, if the periwigged numbers failed to
    fly,
Let babbling dreamers who have also failed
Wait for another age. The time will come
When all he sought and lost shall mount and
    sing.
He saw the life-stream branching out before
    him,
Its forms and colours changing with their sky:
Flocks in the south that lost their warm white
    fleece;
And, in the north, the stubble-coloured hare
Growing snow-white against the winter snows.
The frog that had no jewel in his head,
Except his eyes, was yet a fairy prince,
For he could change the colours of his coat
To match the mud of the stream wherein he
    reigned;
And, if he dwelt in trees, his coat was green.
He saw the green-winged birds of Paraguay
Hardening their beaks upon the shells they
    cracked;
The humming-bird, with beak made needle-
    fine

For sucking honey from long-throated
    blooms;
Finches with delicate beaks for buds of trees,
And water-fowl that, in their age-long plash-
    ing
At the lake's edge, had stretched the films of
    skin
Between their claws to webs. Out through
    the reeds
They rowed at last, and swam to seek their
    prey.
He saw how, in their war against the world,
Myriads of lives mysteriously assumed
The hues that hid them best; the butterfly
    dancing
With its four petals among so many flowers,
Itself a wingèd flower; the hedgerow birds
With greenish backs like leaves, but their soft
    breasts
Light as a downy sky, so that the hawk,
Poised overhead, sees only a vanishing leaf;
Or, if he swoops along the field below
    them,
Loses their silvery flight against the cloud.

He saw the goldfinch, vivid as the blooms
Through which it flutters, as though their
    dews had splashed
Red of the thistle upon its head and throat,
And on its wings the dandelion's gold.
He saw the skylark coloured like its nest
In the dry grass; the partridge, grey and
    brown
In mottled fields, escaping every eye,
Till the foot stumbles over it, and the clump
Of quiet earth takes wing and whirrs away.
I saw him there, a strange and lonely soul,
An eagle in the Swan of Lichfield's pen,
Stretching clipped wings and staring at the
    sky.
He saw the multitudinous hosts of life,
All creatures of the sea and earth and air,
Ascending from one living spiral thread,
Through tracts of time, unreckonable in
    years.
He saw them varying as the plastic clay
Under the Sculptor's hands.
                He saw them flowing
From one Eternal Fount beyond our world,

The inscrutable and indwelling Primal
    Power,
His only *vera causa;* by whose will
There was no gulf between the first and last.
There was no break in that long line of law
Between the first life drifting in the sea,
And man, proud man, the crowning form of
    earth,
Man whose own spine, the framework of his
    pride,
The fern-stem of his life, trunk of his tree,
Sleeps in the fish, the reptile, and the orang,
As all those lives in his own embryo sleep.

What deeper revolution, then, must shake
Those proud ancestral dynasties of earth?
What little man-made temples must go down?
And what august new temple must arise,
One vast cathedral, gargoyled with strange
    life,
Surging through darkness, up to the unknown
    end?

IV

LAMARCK AND CUVIER: THE *VERA CAUSA*

FEAR nothing, Swan of Lichfield. Tuck thy
    head
Beneath thy snowy wing and sleep at ease.
Drift quietly on thy shadowy Minster Pool.
No voice comes yet to shake thy placid world.
Far off—in France—thy wingless angels
    make
Strange havoc, but the bearer of this fire,
The wise physician's unknown comrade, toils
Obscurely now, through his more perilous
    night,
Seeking his *vera causa,* with blind eyes.
Blind, blind as Galileo in his age,
Lamarck embraced his doom and, as in youth,
Held to the post assigned, till Life or Death
Relieved him. All those changes of the world
He had seen more clearly than his unknown
    friend;

And traced their natural order.
He saw the sea-gull like a flake of foam
Tossed from the waves of that creative sea;
The fish that like a speckled patch of sand
Slides over sand upon its broad flat side,
And twists its head until its nether eye
Looks upward, too, and what swam upright
    once
Is fixed in its new shape, and the wry mouth
Grimaces like a gnome at its old foes.
He saw the swarming mackerel shoals that
    swim
Near the crisp surface, rippled with blue and
    green
Round their dark backs to trick the pouncing
    gull,
But silver-bellied to flash like streaks of light
Over the ravenous mouths that from below
Snap at the leaping gleams of the upper sea.
And all these delicate artistries were wrought
By that strange Something-Else which blind
    men call
"Environment," and the name is all their
    need;

A Something-Else that, through the sum of
    things,
Labours unseen; and, for its own strange ends,
Desirous of more swiftness and more strength,
Will teach the hunted deer to escape and fly,
Even while it leads the tiger to pursue.

He saw that sexual war; the stags that fought
In mating-time; the strong confirmed in
    power
By victory. Lust and hunger, pleasure and
    pain,
Like instruments in a dread Designer's hand,
Lured or dissuaded, tempted and transformed.

He saw dark monsters in primeval forests
Tearing the high green branches down for
    food
Age after age, till from their ponderous heads
Out of their own elastic flesh they stretched
A trunk that, like a long grey muscular snake,
Could curl up through the bunches of green
    leaves,
And pluck their food at ease as cattle browse;

THE TORCH-BEARERS

Life's own dark effort aiding that strange
    Power
Without, and all controlled in one great
    plan,
Grotesquely free, and beautifully at one
With law, upsurging to the unknown end.
All Nature like a vast chameleon changed;
And all these forms of life through endless
    years,
Changing, developing, from one filament rose.
Man, on the heights, retravelled in nine moons
All that long journey in little, never to lose
What life had learned on its æonian way:
Man on the heights; but not divided now
From his own struggling kindred of the night.
Few dared to think it yet and set him free
Through knowledge of himself and his own
    power;
Few, yet, in France or England. Let him
    bask
Where in six days God set him at his ease
Among His wingless angels; there to hate
The truth, until he breaks his own vain heart
And finds the law at last and walks with God,

Who, not abhorring even the mire and clay
In the beginning, breathed His life through
    all.
This was his *vera causa.* Hate, contempt,
Ridicule, like a scurrilous wind swooped
    down
From every side. Great Cuvier, with the
    friends
Of orthodoxy, sneered—could species change
Their forms at will? Could the lean tiger's
    need
To crouch in hiding stripe his tawny flesh
With shadows of the cane-break where he
    lay?
Could the giraffe, by wishing for the leaves
Beyond his reach, add to his height one inch?
Or could the reptile's fond desire to fly
Create his wings?
                Could Cuvier read one line
Of this blind man, he might have held his
    peace,
Found his own *versa causa,* and sunk his
    pride;
And even the wiser Darwin, when he came,

Might have withheld his judgment for an
    hour,
And learned from his forerunner. But, in
    their haste,
They flung away his fire; and, as he fell,
They set their heels upon it and stamped it
    out.
Not always does the distant age restore
The balance, or posterity renew
The laurel on the cold dishonoured brow
Unjustly robbed and blindly beaten down.
He laboured on in blindness. At his side
One faithful daughter, labouring with her
    pen,
As he dictated, wrote, month after month,
Year after year; and, when her father died,
She saw him tossed into the general grave,
The pauper's fosse, where none can trace him
    now,
In Montparnasse, but wrapt in deeper peace
Among the unknown and long-forgotten dead.

VIII—IN GERMANY

GOETHE

I

THE DISCOVERER

THE wreathing mist was quietly breathed
    away.
I stood upon a little hill at night;
The tang of pinewoods and the warbling joy
Of hidden brooks was round me.
                    The dark hill
Sloped to a darker garden. On the crest
A wooden cabin rose against the stars.
Its open door, a gap of golden light
In deep blue gloom, told me that he was there.
I saw his darkened house asleep below,
And Weimar clustering round it, a still cloud
Of shadowy slumbering houses.

[215]

THE TORCH-BEARERS

                          Like a shadow,
Tracking the Sun-god to his midnight lair,
I climbed to the lighted cabin on the crest,
And I saw Goethe.

                      At his side a lamp
On a rude table, out of tumbled waves
Of manuscript, like an elfin lighthouse rose.
His bed, a forester's couch for summer
    nights,
Was thrust into a corner. Rows of books
Lined the rough walls.

                A letter was in his hand
From Craigenputtock; and while he looked
    at it,
The unuttered thoughts came flowing into the
    mind
Of his invisible listener—Shadow-of-a-Leaf.
All true, my friend; but there's no halfway
    house.
Rid you of Houndsditch, and you'll not main-
    tain
This quite ungodlike severance of mankind
From Nature and its laws; though I should
    lose

[216]

THE BOOK OF EARTH

My Scots apostle, if I called it so.
What's an apostle? Is it one who sees
Just so much of his hero, as reflects
Himself and his own thoughts? I like him
     well,
And yet he makes me lonelier than before.
Houndsditch may go; but Cuvier will go first;
With all the rest who isolate mankind
From its true place in Nature.
                              Everywhere
I saw the one remodulated form.
The leaf ascended to mysterious bliss
And was assumed, with happy sister-leaves,
Into the heavenly glory of a flower.
Pistil and stamen, calyx and bright crown
Of coloured petals, all were leaves trans-
     formed,
Transfigured, from one type.
                              I saw in man
And his wild kinsfolk of the woods and seas,
In fish and serpent, eagle and orang,
One knotted spine that curled into a skull.
It ran through all their patterns everywhere,
· Playing a thousand variants on one theme,

THE TORCH-BEARERS

Branching through all the frame of fins and
   wings
And spreading through their jointed hands
   and feet.

Throughout this infinite universe I heard
The music of one law.

                              Is man alone
Belied by all the signs of his ascent?
Are men even now so far above the beasts?
What can the tiger teach them when they kill?
Are they so vain that they'd deny the bones
An inch beneath their skin—bones that when
   stripped
Of flesh and mixed with those of their dumb
   kin
Themselves could not distinguish? How they
   clung
To that distinction in the skull of man.
It lacked the inter-maxillary. They grew
   angry
When I foretold it would be found one day.
What's truth to a poet? Back to your dainty
   lies!

[218]

THE BOOK OF EARTH

And then—one day—I found it.
                              Did they say
Strange work for a poet? Is mankind asleep
That it can never feel what then I felt,
To find my faith so quietly confirmed?
I held it in my hand and stared at it,
An eyeless hollow skull that once could think
Its own strange thoughts and stare as well as
        we;
A skull that once was rocked upon a breast,
And looked its deathless love through dying
        eyes;
And, in that skull, above the incisor teeth,
The signs that men denied,—of its ascent
Through endless ages, in the savage night
Of jungle-worlds, before mankind was born.

No thought for poets, and no wonder there?
No gateway to the kingdoms of the mind?
No miracle in the miracle that I saw
Touched, held.
                My body tingled. All my veins
Froze with the inconceivable mystery,
The weirdness and the wonder of it all.

THE TORCH-BEARERS

No vision? And no dream? Let poets play
At bowls with Yorick's relic then, for ever;
Or blow dream-bubbles. I've a world to
    shape;
A law to guide me, and a God to find.

That night in sleep I saw—it was no dream!—
It was too wild, too strange, too darkly true,
And all too human in its monstrous pangs
To be a dream. I saw it, and I live.
I saw, I saw, and closed these eyes to see
That terrible birth in darkness, the black
    night
Of naked agony that first woke the soul.

Night and the jungle, burning with great
    stars,
Rolled all around me. There were steaming
    pools
Of darkness, and the smell of the wild beast
Musky and acrid on the blood-warm air.
The night was like a tiger's hot sweet mouth;
I heard a muffled roar, and a wild cry,
A shriek, a fall.

I saw an uncouth form,
Matted with hair, stretched on the blood-
    stained earth;
And, in the darkness, darker than the night,
Another form uncouth, with matted hair,
Long-armed, like a gorilla, stooping low
Above his mate.
            She did not move or breathe.
He felt her body with his long-clawed hands,
And called to her—a harsh, quick, startled
    cry.
She did not hear. One arm was tightly wound
About her little one. Both were strangely
    still,
Stiller than sleep.
            He squatted down to wait.
They did not move all night. At dawn he
    stood
By that stiff mockery. He stretched up his
    arms
And clutched at the red sun that mocked him,
    too.
Then, out of his blind heart, with one fierce
    pang,

THE TORCH-BEARERS

The man-child, Grief, was born.
                                His round dark eyes
Pricked with strange brine, and his broad
    twitching mouth
Quivered. He fell on the dark unanswering
    earth
Beside his dead, with inarticulate cries,
Great gasping sobs that seemed to rend his
    flesh
And shook him through and through.
The night returned and, with the night, a
    hope,
Because he could not see their staring eyes.
He rushed into the jungle and returned
With fruits and berries, ripe and soft and red.
He rubbed the dark wet plums against their
    lips.
He smeared the juices on their locked white
    teeth;
Pleading with little murmurs, while the stars
Wheeled overhead, and velvet-footed beasts
Approached and stared with eyes of gold and
    green;
And even the little leaves were all alive;

And tree-toads chirruped; but those dark
  forms lay still.

Day followed night. He did not know them
  now.
All that had been so swift to answer him
Was gone. But whither? Every day he saw
A ball of light arising in the East
And moving overhead the self-same way.
Into the West. . . .
The strange new hunger eating at his heart
Urged him to follow it, stumbling blindly on
Through endless forests; but it moved so
  swiftly
He could not overtake it, could not reach
The place where it went down, ere darkness
  came.
Then—in the dark—a shadow sometimes
  moved
Before him, like the shadow he had lost,
And with a cry, *Yoo! Yoo!* he would awake
And, crashing through the forests to the West,
Would try to steal a march upon the sun,
And see it rise inexorably behind him,

And sail above, inexorably, at noon,
And sink beyond, inexorably, at night.

Then, after many suns had risen and set,
He saw at dusk a blaze of crimson light
Between the thinning tree-trunks and emerged
Out of the forest into a place of rocks,
Washed by a water greater than the world.
He stood, an uncouth image carved in stone,
Staring into the West. He saw the sun
Staining the clouds and sinking into the flood.
His lips were parched with thirst, a deeper
     thirst
Than any spring on earth could quench again;
And when he laid him down upon the shore
To drink of that deep water, he knew well
That he was nearer now to what he sought,
Because it tasted salt as his lost tears.

He drank. He waded out, and drank again.
Then a big wave of darkness rushed upon
     him,
And rolled him under. He rose, and with
     great arms

THE BOOK OF EARTH

Swam out into that boundless flood of brine
Towards the last glimmer of light; a dark,
    blind brute,
Sobbing and panting, till the merciful waves,
Salt in his eyes and salt upon his lips,
Had drawn the agony out of his labouring
    limbs
And gently as the cradling boughs that once
Rocked him to sleep, embraced and drew him
    down
Into oblivion, the first life that caught
With eyes bewildered by the light they knew,
A glimpse of the unknown light beyond the
    world.

II

THE PROPHET

BEFORE the first wild matins of the thrush
Had ended, or the sun sucked up the dew,
I saw him wrestling with his thoughts.   He
    rose,
Laid down that eagle's feather in his hand,
And looked at his own dawn.
                              He did not speak.
Only the secret music of his mind
In an enchanted silence flowed to meet
The listener, as his own great morning flowed
Through those Æolian pinewoods at his feet.
Colours and forms of earth and heaven you
    flow
Like clouds around a star—the streaming robe
Of an Eternal Glory.   Let the law
Of Beauty, in your rhythmic folds, by night
And day, through all the universe, reveal
The way of the unseen Mover to these eyes.

THE BOOK OF EARTH

Last night I groped into the dark abyss
Under the feet of man, and saw Thee there
Ascending, from that depth below all depth.
O, now, at dawn, as I look up to heaven
Descend to meet me, on my upward way.
How shall they grasp Thy glory who despise
The law that is Thy kingdom here on earth,
Our way of freedom and our path to Thee?
How shall they grasp that law, or rightly
        know
One truth in Nature, who deny Thy Power,
Unresting and unhasting, everywhere?
How shall the seekers, bound to their own
        tasks,
Each following his own quest, each spying out
His fragment of a truth, reintegrate
Their universe and behold all things in one?
Be this the task of Song, then, to renew
That universal vision in the soul.
Rise, poet, to thy universal height,
Then stoop, as eagles do from their wide
        heaven
On their particular prey. Between the clouds
They see more widely and truly than the mole

At work in his dark tunnel, though he cast
His earth upon the fields they watch afar.
Work on, inductive mole; but there's a use
In that too lightly abandoned way of thought,
The way of Plato, and the way of Christ,
That man must find again, ere he can build
The temple of true knowledge. Those who
  trust
To Verulam's *Novum Organum* alone,
Never can build it. Quarriers of the truth,
They cut the stones, but cannot truly lay them;
For only he whose deep remembering mind
Holds the white archetype, can to music build
His towers, from the pure pattern imprinted
  there.
He, and he only, in one timeless flash
Through all this moving universe discerns
The inexorable sequences of law,
And, in the self-same flash, transfiguring
  all,
Uniting and transcending all, beholds
With my Spinoza's own ecstatic eyes
God in the hidden law that fools call
  "chance,"

THE BOOK OF EARTH

God in the star, the flower, the moondrawn
  wave,
God in the snake, the bird, and the wild beast,
God in that long ascension from the dark,
God in the body and in the soul of man,
God uttering life, and God receiving death.

IX—IN ENGLAND

DARWIN

I

CHANCE AND DESIGN

" *I AM the whisper that he ceased to hear,"*
    The quiet voice of Shadow-of-a-Leaf
      began;
And, as he spoke, the flowing air before me
Shone like a crystal sphere, wherein I saw
All that he pictured, through his own deep
    eyes.

I waited in his garden there, at Down.
I peered between the crooklights of a hedge
Where ragged robins grew.
               Far off, I heard
The clocklike rhythm of an ironshod staff
Clicking on gravel, clanking on a flint.

THE TORCH-BEARERS

Then, round the sand-walk, under his trees he
    strode,
A tall lean man, wrapt in a loose dark cloak,
His big soft hat of battered sun-burnt straw
Pulled down to shade his face. But I could
    see,
For I looked upward, the dim brooding
    weight
Of silent thought that soon would shake the
    world.

He paused to watch an ant upon its way.
He bared his head. I saw the shaggy brows
That like a mountain-fortress overhung
The deep veracious eyes, the dogged face
Where kindliness and patience, knowledge,
    power,
And pain quiescent under the conquering
    will,
In that profound simplicity which marks
The stature of the mind, the truth of art,
The majesty of every natural law.
The child's wise innocence, and the silent
    worth

Of human grief and love, had set their seal.

I stole behind him, and he did not hear
Or see me. I was only Shadow-of-a-Leaf;
And yet—I knew the word was on its way
That might annul his life-work in an hour.
I heard the whisper of every passing wing
Where, wrapt in peace, among the hills of
      Kent,
The patient watchful intellect had prepared
A mightier revolution for mankind
Even than the world-change of Copernicus
When the great central earth began to move
And dwine to a grain of dust among the stars.
I saw him pondering over a light-winged seed
That floated, like an elfin aeronaut,
Across the path. He caught it in his hand
And looked at it. He touched its delicate
      hooks
And set it afloat again. He watched it sailing,
Carrying its tiny freight of life away
Over the quick-set hedge, up, into the hills.
I heard him muttering, "beautiful! Surely
      this

[233]

Implies design!

        Design?" Then, from his face
The wonder faded, and he shook his head;
But with such reverence and humility
That his denial almost seemed a prayer.

A prayer—for, not long after, in his house,
I saw him bowed, the first mind of his age,
Bowed, helpless, by the deathbed of his child;
Pondering, with all that knowledge, all that
      power,
Powerless, and ignorant of the means to save;
A dumb Prometheus, bending his great head
In silence, as he drank those broken words
Of thanks, the pitiful thanks of small parched
      lips,
For a sip of water, a smile, a cooling hand
On the hot brow; thanks for his goodness—
      God!
Thanks from a dying child, just ten years old!

And, while he stood in silence by her grave,
Hearing the ropes creak as they lowered her
      down

[234]

THE BOOK OF EARTH

Into the cold dark hollow, while he breathed
The smell of the moist earth, those calm
    strange words—
I am the Resurrection and the Life,
Echoed and echoed through his lonely
    mind,
Only to deepen his agony of farewell
Into Eternity.
              Dumbly there he strove
To understand how accents so divine,
In words so worthy of eternal power,
So postulant of it in their calm majesty,
Could breathe through mortal lips.
                 Madman or God,
Who else could say them?
                  God it could not be,
If in his mortal blindness he saw clear;
And yet, and yet, could madness wring the
    heart
Thus, thus, and thus, for nineteen hundred
    years?
*Would that she knew, would God that she
    knew now,*
How much we loved her!

THE TORCH-BEARERS

                    The blind world, still ruled
By shams, and following in hypnotic flocks
The sheep-bell of an hour, still thought of
    him
"The Man of Science" as less or more than
    man,
Coldly aloof from love and grief and pain;
Held that he knew far more, and felt far less
Than other men, and, even while it praised
The babblers for their reticence and their
    strength,
The shallow for their depth, the blind for
    sight,
The rattling weathercocks for their love of
    truth,
Ere long would brand, as an irreverent fool,
This great dumb simple man, with his bowed
    head.

Could the throng see that drama, as I saw it—
I, Shadow-of-a-Leaf,—could the blind throng
    discern
The true gigantic drama of those hours
Among the quiet hills as, one by one,

THE BOOK OF EARTH

His facts fell into place; their broken edges
Joined, like the fragments of a vast mosaic,
And, slowly, the new picture of the world,
Emerging in majestic pageantry
Out of the primal dark, before him grew;
Grew by its own inevitable law;
Grew, and earth's ancient fantasies dwindled
    down;
The stately fabric of the old creation
Crumbled away; while man, proud demi-
    god,
Stripped of all arrogance now, priest, beggar,
    king,
Captive and conqueror, all must own alike
Their ancient lineage. Kin to the dumb
    beasts
By the red life that flowed through all their
    veins
From hearts of the same shape, beating all as
    one
In man and brute; kin, by those kindred
    forms
Of flesh and bone, with eyes and ears and
    mouths

THE TORCH-BEARERS

That saw and heard and hungered like his
    own,
His mother Earth reclaimed him.
                   Back and back,
He traced them, till the last faint clue died
    out
In lifeless earth and sea.
                I watched him striving
To follow further, bending his great brows
Over the intense lens. . . .
                Far off, I heard
The murmur of human life, laughter and
    weeping;
Heard the choked sobbings by a million
    graves,
And saw a million faces, wrung with grief,
Lifted forlornly to the Inscrutable Power.

I saw him raise his head. I heard his thought
As others hear a whisper—*Surely this
Implies design!*
             And worlds on aching worlds
Of dying hope were wrapped in those four
    words.

He stared before him, wellnigh overwhelmed
For one brief moment, with instinctive awe
Of Something that . . . determined every
    force
Directed every atom. . . .
                  Then, in a flash,
The indwelling vision vanished at the voice
Of his own blindfold reason. For what
    mind
Could so unravel the complicated threads,
The causes that are caused by the effects
Of other causes, intricately involved,
Woven and interwoven, in endless mazes,
Wandering through infinite time, infinite
    space,
And yet, an ordered and mysterious whole,
Before whose very being all mortal power
Must abdicate its sovereignty?
                  A dog
Might sooner hope to leap beyond the mind
Of Newton than a man might hope to
    grasp
Even in this little whirl of earth and sun
The Scheme of the All-determining Absolute.

And yet—if that—the All-moving, were the
    One
Reality, and sustained and made all forms,
Then, by the self-same power in man himself
Whatever was real in man might understand
That same Reality, being one substance with
    it,
One substance with the essential Soul of all,—
Might understand, as children understand,
Even in ignorance, those who love them best;
Might recognise, as through their innocent
    eyes,
The highest, which is Love, though all the
    worlds
Of lesser knowledge passed unheeded by.
What meant those moments else? Moments
    that came
And went on wings, wild as these wings of
    mine,
The wings of Shadow-of-a-Leaf,
Quick with a light that never could be
    reached
By toiling up the mountain-sides of thought;
Consummate meanings that were never found

THE BOOK OF EARTH

By adding units; moments of strange awe
When that majestic sequence of events
We call the cosmos, from its wheeling atoms
Up to its wheeling suns, all spoke one Power,
One Presence, One Unknowable, and One
    Known?

*In the beginning God made heaven and
    earth:*
He, too, believed it, once. . . .

II

THE VOYAGE

               As if the wings
Of Shadow-of-a-Leaf had borne me through
    the West
So that the sunset changed into the dawn,
I saw him in his youth.

               The large salt wind,
The creak of cordage, the wild swash of waves
Were round him as he paced the clear white
    deck,
An odd loose-tweeded sojourner, in a world
Of uniforms and guns.

               The *Beagle* plunged
Westward, upon the road that Drake had
    sailed;
But this new voyager, on a longer quest,
Sailed on a stranger sea; and, though I heard
His ringing laugh, he seemed to live apart
In his own mind, from all who moved around
    him.

THE BOOK OF EARTH

I saw him while the *Beagle* basked at anchor
Under West Indian palms. He lounged there,
    tanned
With sun; tall, lankier in his cool white drill;
The big slouched straw pulled down to shade
    his eyes.
The stirring wharf was one bright haze of
    colour;
Kaleidoscopic flakes, orange and green,
Blood-red and opal, glancing to and fro,
Through purple shadows. The warm air
    smelt of fruit.

He leaned his elbows on the butt of a gun
And listened, while a red-faced officer,
    breathing
Faint whiffs of rum, expounded lazily,
With loosely stumbling tongue, the cynic's
    code
His easy rule of life, belying the creed
That both professed.
                    And, in one flash, I caught
A glimpse of something deeper, missed by
    both,—

THE TORCH-BEARERS

The subtle touch of the Master-Ironist
Unfolding his world-drama, point by point,
In every sight and sound and word and
    thought,
Packed with significance.

                Out of its myriad scenes
All moving swiftly on, unguessed by man,
To close in one great climax of clear light,
This vivid moment flashed.

                The cynic ceased;
And Darwin, slowly knitting his puzzled
    brows,
Answered, *"But it is wrong!"*
"Wrong?" chuckled the other. "Why should
    it be wrong?"
And Darwin, Darwin,—he that was to grasp
The crumbling pillars of their infidel Temple
And bring them headlong down to the honest
    earth,
Answered again, naïvely as a child,
"Does not the Bible say so?"

                A broad grin
Wreathed the red face that stared into his
    own;

And, later, when the wardroom heard the
      jest,
The same wide grin from Christian mouth to
      mouth
Spread like the ripples on a single pool
Quietly enough! They liked him. They'd
      not hurt him!
And Darwin, strange, observant, simple soul,
Saw clearly enough; had eyes behind his back
For every smile; though in his big slow
      mind
He now revolved a thought that greatly puz-
      zled him,
A thought that, in their light sophistication,
These humorists had not guessed.
                         Once, in his cabin,
His red-faced cynic had picked up a book
By one whose life was like a constant light
On the high altar of Truth.
                         He had read a page,
Then flung it down, with a contemptuous
      oath,
Muttering, "These damned atheists! Why
      d'you read them?"

Could pagan minds be stirred, then, to such
    wrath
Because the man they called an "atheist"
    smiled
At dates assigned by bland ecclesiasts
To God for His creation?

            Man was made
On March the ninth, at ten o'clock in the
    morning
(*A Tuesday*), *just six thousand years ago:*
A legend of a somewhat different cast
From that deep music of the first great
    phrase
In *Genesis.* The strange irony here struck
    home.
For Darwin, here, was with the soul-bowed
    throng
Of prophets, while the ecclesiasts blandly
    toyed
With little calendars, which his "atheist's
    book,"
In its irreverence, whispered quite away;
Whispered (for all such atheists bend their
    heads

THE BOOK OF EARTH

Doubtless in shame) that, in the Book of
    Earth,
Six thousand years were but as yesterday,
A flying cloud, a shadow, a breaking wave.
Million of years were written upon the rocks
That told its history. To upheave one range
Of mountains, out of the sea that had sub-
    merged
So many a continent, ere mankind was born,
The harnessed forces, governed all by law,
Had laboured, dragging down and building
    up,
Through distances of Time, unthinkable
As those of starry space.
                  It dared to say
(This book so empty of mystery and awe!)
That, searching the dark scripture of the
    rocks,
It found therein no sign of a beginning,
No prospect of an end.
               Strange that the Truth,
Whether upheld by the pure law within
Or by the power of reason, thus dismayed
These worshippers of a little man-made code.

Alone there in his cabin, with the books
Of Humboldt, Lyell, Herschel, spread before
    him.
He made his great decision.

                     If the realm
Beyond the bounds of human knowledge gave
So large a sanctuary to mortal lies,
Henceforth his Bible should be one inscribed
Directly with the law—the Book of Earth.

III

THE TESTIMONY OF THE ROCKS

I SAW him climbing like a small dark speck
—Fraught with what vast significance to the
    world—
Among the snow-capt Andes, a dark point
Of travelling thought, alone upon the heights,
To watch the terrible craters as they breathed
Their smouldering wrath against the sky.
                         I saw him,
Pausing above Portillo's pass to hear
The sea-like tumult, where brown torrents
    rolled
Innumerable thousands of rough stones,
Jarring together, and hurrying all one way.
He stood there, spellbound, listening to the
    voice
Of Time itself, the moments hurrying by
For ever irrecoverably. I heard
His very thought. The stones were on their
    way

THE TORCH-BEARERS

To the ocean that had made them; every note
In their wild music was a prophecy
Of continents unborn.

               When he had seen
Those continents in embryo, beds of sand
And shingle, cumulant on the coastwise
    plains,
Thousands of feet in thickness, he had
    doubted
Whether the river of time itself could grind
And pile such masses there. But when he
    heard
The mountain-torrents rattling, he recalled
How races had been born and passed away,
And night and day, through years unreckon-
    able,
These grinding stones had never ceased to
    roll
On their steep course. Not even the Cordil-
    leras,
Had they been ribbed with adamant, could
    withstand
That slow sure waste. Even those majestic
    heights

Would vanish. Nothing—not the wind that
    blows
Was more unstable than the crust of the earth.

He landed at Valdivia, on the day
When the great earthquake shuddered
    through the hills
From Valparaiso, southward to Cape Horn.
I saw him wandering through a ruined city
Of Paraguay, and measuring on the coast
The upheaval of new land, discovering rocks
Ten feet above high-water, rocks with shells
For which the dark-eyed panic-stricken
    throngs
Had dived at ebb, a few short days ago.
I saw him—strange discoverer—as he sailed
Through isles, not only uncharted, but new-
    born,
Isles newly arisen and glistening in the sun,
And atolls where he thought an older height
Had sunk below the smooth Pacific sea.

He explored the Pampas; and before him
    passed

THE TORCH-BEARERS

The centuries that had made them; the great
    streams
Gathering the red earth at their estuaries
In soft rich deltas, till new plains of loam
Over the Banda granite slowly spread,
And seeds took root and mightier forests tow-
    ered,
Forests that human foot could never tread,
Forests that human eye could never see;
But by the all-conquering human mind at last
Trodden and seen, waving their leaves in air
As at an incantation,
And filled once more with monstrous forms
    of life.

He found their monstrous bones embedded
    there,
And, as he found them, all those dry bones
    lived.
I stole beside him in the dark, and heard,
In the unfathomable forest deeps, the crash
Of distant boughs, a wild and lonely sound,
Where Megatherium, the gigantic Sloth
Whose thigh was thrice an elephant's in girth,

THE BOOK OF EARTH

Rose, blindly groping, and with armoured
  hands
Tore down the trees to reach their tender
  crests
And strip them of their more delicious green.
I saw him pondering on the secret bond
Between the living creatures that he found
On the main coast, and those on lonely isles;
Forms that diverged, and yet were closely
  akin.
One key, one only, unlocked the mystery there.

Unless God made, for every separate isle
As it arose, new tribes of plants, birds, beasts,
In variant images of the tribes He set
Upon their nearest continent, grading all
By time, and place, and distance from the
  shore,
The bond between them was the bond of
  blood.
All, all had branched from one original tree.

I saw him off the Patagonian coast
Staring at something stranger than a dream.
There, on a rocky point above the ship

With its world-voyaging thoughts, he first be-
    held
Primeval man. There, clustering on the crags,
Backed by their echoing forests of dark beech,
The naked savages yelled at the white sails,
Like wolves that bay the moon. They tossed
    their arms
Wildly through their long manes of stream-
    ing hair,
Like troubled spirits from an alien world.
Whence had they risen? From what ances-
    tral night?
What bond of blood was there? What dread-
    ful Power
Begot them—fallen or risen—from heaven or
    hell?

I saw him hunting everywhere for light
On life's dark mystery; gathering everywhere
Armies of fact, that pointed all one way,
And yet—what *vera causa* could he find
In blindfold Nature?

                    Even had he found it,
What æons would be needed! Earth was old;

THE BOOK OF EARTH

But could the unresting loom of infinite time
Weave this wild miracle, or evolve one nerve
Of all this intricate network in the brain,
This exquisite machine that looked through
    heaven,
Revelled in colours of a sunset sky,
Or met love's eyes on earth?
                      Everywhere, now,
He found new clues that led him all one way.
And, everywhere, in the record of the rocks,
Time and to spare for all that Time could do,
But not his *vera causa*.
                  Earth grew strange.
Even in the ghostly gleam that told the watch
One daybreak that the ship was nearing home
He saw those endless distances again. . . .
He saw through mist, over the struggling
    waves
That run between the white-chalk cliffs of
    France
And England, sundered coasts that once were
    joined
And clothed with one wide forest.
                   The deep sea

Had made the strange white body of that
  broad land,
Beautifully establishing it on death,
Building it, inch by inch, through endless
  years
Out of innumerable little gleaming bones,
The midget skeletons of the twinkling tribes
That swarmed above in the more lucid green
Ten thousand fathoms nearer to the sun.
There they lived out their gleam of life and
  died,
Then slowly drifted down into the dark,
And spread in layers upon the cold sea-bed
The invisible grains and flakes that were their
  bones.
Layer on layer of flakes and grains of lime,
Where life could never build, they built it up
By their incessant death. Though but an inch
In every thousand years, they built it up,
Inch upon inch, age after endless age;
And the dark weight of the incumbent Deep
Compressed them (Power determined by
  what Will?)
Out of the night that dim creation rose

THE BOOK OF EARTH

The seas withdrew. The bright new land ap-
    peared.
Then Gaul and Albion, nameless yet, were
    one;
And the wind brought a myriad wingèd seeds,
And the birds carried them, and the forests
    grew,
And through their tangled ways the tall elk
    roared.
But sun and frost and rain, the grinding
    streams
And rhythmic tides (the tools of what dread
    Hand?)
Still laboured on; till, after many a change,
The great moon-harnessed energies of the
    sea
Came swinging back, the way of the southwest
    wind,
And, æon after æon, hammering there,
Rechannelled through that land their shining
    way.
There all those little bones now greet the sun
In gleaming cliffs of chalk; and, in their
    chines

[257]

The chattering jackdaw builds, while over-
 head
On the soft mantle of turf the violet wakes
In March, and young-eyed lovers look for
 Spring.
What of the Cause? O, no more rounded
 creeds
Framed in a realm where no man could re-
 fute them!
Honesty, honesty, honesty, first of all.
And so he turned upon the world around him,
The same grave eyes of deep simplicity
With which he had faced his pagan-christian
 friends
And quoted them their Bible. . . .
Slowly he marshalled his worldwide hosts of
 fact,
Legions new-found, or first assembled now,
In their due order. Lyell had not dared
To tell the truth he knew. He found in earth
The records of its vanished worlds of life,
Each with its own strange forms, in its own
 age,
Sealed in its own rock-system.

THE BOOK OF EARTH

In the first,
The rocks congealed from fire, no sign of life;
And, through the rest, in order as they were
    made,
From oldest up to youngest, first the signs
Of life's first gropings; then, in gathering
    power,
Strange fishes, lizards, birds, and uncouth
    beasts,
Worlds of strange life, but all in ordered
    grades,
World over world, each tombed in its own age
Or merging into the next with subtle changes,
Delicate modulations of one form,
(Urged by what force? Impelled by what
    dark power?)
Progressing upward, into subtler forms
Through all the buried strata, till there came
Forms that still live, still fight for life on
    earth,
Tiger and wolf and ape; and, last of all,
The form of man; the child of yesterday.
Of yesterday! For none had ever found
Among the myriad forms of older worlds,

Locked in those older rocks through tracts of
    time
Out-spanning thought, one vestige of man-
    kind.
There was no human footprint on the shores
Whose old compacted sand, now turned to
    stone,
Still showed the ripples where a summer
    sea
Once whispered, ere the mastodon was born.
There were the pitted marks, all driven one
    way,
That showed how raindrops fell, and the
    west wind blew.
There on the naked stone remained the tracks
Where first the sea-beasts crawled out of the
    sea,
A few salt yards upon the long dark trail
That led through æons to the tidal roar
Of lighted cities and this world of tears.
The shell, the fern, the bird's foot, the beast's
    claw,
Had left their myriad signs.   Their forms re-
    mained,

Their delicate whorls, their branching fronds,
    their bones,
Age after age, like jewels in the rocks;
But, till the dawning of an age so late,
It seemed like yesterday, no sign, no trace,
No relic of mankind!
              Then, in that age
Among the skulls, made equal in the grave,
Of ape and wolf, last of them all, looked up
That naked shrine with its receding brows,
And its two sightless holes, the skull of man.
Round it, his tools and weapons, the chipped
    flints,
The first beginnings of his fight for power,
The first results of his first groping thought
Proclaimed his birth, the youngest child of
    time.
Born, and not made? Born—of what lesser
    life?
Was man so arrogant that he could disdain
The words he used so glibly of his God—
Born, and not made?
            Could Lyell, who believed
That, in the world around us, we should find

THE TORCH-BEARERS

The self-same causes and the self-same laws
To-day as yesterday; and throughout all time;
And that the Power behind all changes works
By law alone; law that includes all heights,
All depths, of reason, harmony, and love;
Could Lyell hold that all those realms of life,
Each sealed apart in its own separate age,
With its own separate species, had been called
Suddenly, by a special Act of God,
Out of the void and formless? Could he think
Even that mankind, this last emergent form,
After so many æons of ordered law,
Was by miraculous Hands in one wild hour,
Suddenly kneaded out of the formless clay?
And was the formless clay more noble, then,
Than this that breathed, this that had eyes to
    see,
This whose dark heart could beat, this that
    could die?
No! Lyell knew that this wild house of flesh
Was never made by hands, not even those
    Hands;
And that to think so were to discrown God,
And not to crown Him, as the blind believed.

THE BOOK OF EARTH

The miracle was a vaster than they knew.
The law by which He worked was all un-
    known;
Subtler than music, quieter than light,
The mighty process that through countless
    changes,
Delicate grades and tones and semi-tones,
Out of the formless slowly brought forth
    forms,
Lifeless as crystals, or translucent globes
Drifting in water; till, through endless years,
Out of their myriad changes, one or two
More subtle in combination, at the touch
Of light began to move, began to attract
Substances that could feed them; blindly at
    first;
But as an artist, with all heaven for prize,
Pores over every syllable, tests each thread
Of his most tenuous thought, the moving
    Power
Spent endless æons of that which men call
    Time,
To form one floating tendril that could close
On what it touched.

[263]

Who whispered in his ear
That fleeting thought?
We must suppose a Power
Intently watching—through all the universe—
Each slightest variant, seizing on the best,
Selecting them, as men by conscious choice
In their small realm selected and reshaped
Their birds and flowers.
We must suppose a Power
In that immense night-cleaving pageantry
Which men call Nature, a selective Power,
Choosing through æons as men choose
through years.

Many are called, few chosen, quietly breathed
Shadow-of-a-Leaf, in exquisite undertone
One phrase of the secret music. . . .
He did not hear.
Lamarck—all too impatiently he flung
Lamarck aside; forgetting how in days
When the dark Book of Earth was darker yet
Lamarck had spelled gigantic secrets out,
And left an easier task for the age to come;
Forgetting more than this; for Darwin's mind,

[264]

THE BOOK OF EARTH

Working at ease in Nature, lost its way
In history, and the thoughts of other men.
For him Lamarck had failed, and he misread
His own forerunner's mind. Blindfold de-
    sires
Had never shaped a wing. The grapevine's
    need
To cling and climb could thrust no tendrils
    out.
The environing snows of Greenland could not
    cloak
Its little foxes with their whiter fur.
Nor could the wing-shut butterfly's inner will
Mimic the shrivelled leaf on the withered
    bough
So cunningly that the bird might perch beside
    it
And never see its prey.
                    Was it blind chance
That flashed his own great fragment of the
    truth
Into his mind? What *vera causa,* then,
What leap of Nature brought that truth to
    birth,

[265]

THE TORCH-BEARERS

Illumining all the world?
                    It flashed upon him
As at a sudden contact of two wires
The current flashes through; or, when through
        space,
A meteorite for endless ages rolls
In darkness, and its world of night appears
Unchangeable for ever, till, all at once,
It plunges into a soft resisting sea
Of planet-girdling air, and burns with heat,
And bursts into a blaze, while far below,
Two lovers, in a world beyond its ken,
Look from a little window into the night
And see a falling star.
                        By such wild light,
An image of his own ambiguous "chance,"
Which was not "chance," but governed by a
        law
Unknown, too vast for men to comprehend
(Too vast for any to comprehend but One,
Breathed Shadow-of-a-Leaf, who in each part
        discerns
Its harmony with the whole), at last the clue
Flashed on him. . . .

THE BOOK OF EARTH

In the strange ironical scheme
Wherein he moved, of the Master-Dramatist,
It was his own ambiguous "chance" that slipt
A book of Malthus into his drowsy hand
And drew his drowsy eyes down to that law
Of struggling men and nations.

Was it "chance"
That in this intricate torch-race tossed him
    there
Light from one struggling on an alien track
And yet not alien, since all roads to truth
Meet in one goal at last?

Was it blind chance
That even in this triumphant flash prepared
The downfall of his human pride, and slipt
The self-same volume into another hand;
And, in the lonely islands of Malay,
Drew Wallace to the self-same page, and said
—Though only Shadow-of-a-Leaf could hear
    that voice,—
Whose is the kingdom, whose the glory and
    power?

O, exquisite irony of the Master, there

THE TORCH-BEARERS

Unseen by both, their generous rivalry
Evolved, perfected, the new thought for man;
And, over both, and all their thoughts, a
     Power
Intently watching, made of their struggle for
     truth
An image of the law that they illumed.

So all that wasting of a myriad seeds
In Nature's wild profusion was not waste,
Not even such waste as drives the flying grains
Under the sculptor's chisel, but was itself
A cause of that unending struggle of life
Through which all life ascends.
                              The conqueror there
Was chosen by laws inexorably precise,
As though to infinite Reason infinite Art
Were wedded, and had found in infinite
     "chance"
Full scope for their consummate certainties,—
Choice and caprice, freedom and law in one.
Each slightest variant, in a myriad ways,
That armed or shielded or could help its kind,
Would lead to a new triumph; would reveal,

[268]

THE BOOK OF EARTH

In varying, subtler ways of varying still;
New strokes of that divinest "chance" of all
Which poet and sculptor count as unforeseen,
And unforeseeable; yet, when once achieved,
They recognise as crowning law with law,
And witnessing to infinitudes of Power
In that creative Will which shapes the world.
O, in that widening splendour of the mind,
Blinder than Buffon, blinder than Lamarck,
His eyes amazed with all that leapt to light,
Dazed with a myriad details, lost the whole.
He saw the law whereby the few were chosen
From forms already at variance. Back and
      back
He traced his law, and every step was true.
And yet his *vera causa* was no Cause,
For it determined nothing. It revealed,
In part, how subtler variants had arisen
From earliest simpler variants, but no more.

*   *   *   *   *   *   *

Subtler than music, quieter than light,
The Power that wrought those changes; and
      the last
Were all implied and folded in the first,

THE TORCH-BEARERS

As the gnarled oak-tree with its thousand
    boughs
Writhing to heaven and striking its grim roots
Like monstrous talons into the mountain's
    heart
Is pent in one smooth acorn. So each life,
In little, retold the tale; each separate man
Was, in himself, the world's epitome,
A microcosm, wherein who runs may read
The history of the whole; from the first seed
Enclosed in the blind womb, until life wake
Through moons or æons of embryonic change
To human thought and love, and those desires
Which still grope upward, into the unknown
    realms
As far beyond us now as Europe lay
From the first life that crawled out of the sea.

There lies our hope; but O, the endless way!
And the lost road of knowledge, endless, too!
That infinite hope was not for him. One life
Hardly sufficed for his appointed task,
To find on earth his clues to the unknown law,
Out-miracling all miracles had he known,

THE BOOK OF EARTH

Whereby this lifeless earth, so clearly seen
Across the abyss of time, this lifeless earth
Washed by a lifeless ocean, by no power
But that which moves within the things we
    see,
Swept the blind rocks into the cities of men,
With great cathedrals towering to the sky,
And little ant-like swarms in their dark aisles
Kneeling to that Unknowable.

                     His to trace
The way by inches, never to see the whole,
Never to grasp the miracle in the law,
And wrestling with it, to be written by light
As by an Angel's finger in the dark.
Could he have stood on that first lifeless coast
With Shadow-of-a-Leaf, and seen that lifeless
    brine,
Rocks where no mollusc clung, nor seaweed
    grew;
Could he have heard a whisper,—*Only wait.*
Be patient. On one sure and certain day,
Out of the natural changes of these rocks
And seas, at last, a great ship will go by;
Cities will dusk that heaven; and you shall see

THE TORCH-BEARERS

Two lovers pass, reading one printed book,
The Paradiso. . . .
                Would he have been so sure
That Nature had no miracles in her heart
More inconceivably shattering to the mind
Than madness ever dreamed?   For this, this,
    this,
Had happened, though the part obscured the
    whole;
And his own labour, in a myriad ways,
Endlessly linking part to part, had lost
The *vera causa* that Lamarck had known,
The one determining Cause that moved
    through all.

IV

THE PROTAGONISTS

THE mist cleared. As an airman flying, I
    saw,
Between the quiet wings of Shadow-of-a-
    Leaf,
Far down, a coiling glitter of willowy
    streams,
Then grey remembered battlements that en-
    closed
Gardens, like nests of nightingales; a bridge;
An airy tower; a shadowy dome; the High;
St Mary's delicate spire.
                  A sound of bells
Rose like a spray of melody from the far
Diminished fountains of the City of Youth.
I heard and almost wept.
               The walls grew large
And soared to meet me. As the patterned
    streets

[273]

THE TORCH-BEARERS

Break into new dimensions, passing from sight
While the airman glides and circles down,
 they rose,
And the outer City, vanishing, revealed
The secret life within. At once I passed
Through walls of stone on those ethereal
 wings;
And, as an unseen spirit might survey
A crowded theatre from above, I saw
A packed assembly, gazing, hushed and still,
At certain famous leaders of that hour
On their raised daïs. Henslow in the midst,
Their president, gentle, tolerant, reverent,
 kind,
Darwin's old tutor, scientist and half-saint;
Owen beside him, crabbèd as John Knox,
And dry as his dead bones; bland Wilber-
 force,
The great smooth Bishop of Oxford, pledged
 and primed
To make an end of Darwin, once for all.
Not far away, a little in shadow, sat
A strange young man, tall, slight, with keen
 dark eyes,

Who might, in the irresponsible way of youth,
Defend an absent thinker. Let him beware.
There was a balance of power in science, too,
Which would resent disturbance. He'd be
     crushed
By sheer weight of authority, then set,
Duly submissive, in his proper place.
His name was Huxley.
                              A square close-crowded room,
It held, in little, a concentrated world,
Imaging, on a microcosmic stage,
The doubts, the fears, the jealousies, and dull
     hates
That now beset one lonely soul at Down;
But imaging, also, dauntless love of truth
In two or three, the bearers of the fire.

Henslow, subdued, with twenty reticent words
That, in their mere formality, seemed aware
Of silent dark momentous currents flowing
Under the trivial ripple of use and wont,
Called on Daubeny, first, for his discourse
On Sex in Flowers, and their descent through
     time.

Daubeny, glancing over his glasses, bowed
And twinkled a wise physician's rosy smile,
As one of his many parts; an all-round man,
Sound Latinist and an excellent judge of wine,
Humanist and geologist, who had tracked
Guettard through all his craters in Auvergne,
And, afterwards, with a map in his right hand,
And Ovid's 'Ars Amoris' in his left,
Traced the volcanic chains through Hungary,
Italy, Transylvania, and returned
To Oxford, as her botanist at the last,
With silvery hair, but otherwise unchanged,
Oxford in bloom and Oxford to the core.
Swimming serene in academic air,
With open mind and non-committal phrase
He proved he knew how little all men know;
And whoso kept that little to himself
Could never be caught tripping.
                                        Then he smiled,
And so remained the wisest of them all.

For half an hour the sexes of the flowers
Danced from his learned discourse, through
    the minds

Of half his feminine hearers, like a troop
Of Bacchanals, blowing kisses.

                                 In the crowd
I saw, at the whimsical chuckle of Shadow-of-
    a-Leaf,
The large-eyed spinster with the small pursed
    mouth,
Eliza Pym of Woodstock, who desired
To know about the wild flowers that she
    drew
In delicate water-colours for her friends.
She sat bolt upright, innocently amazed
And vaguely trepidant in her hooped green
    gown.
What? Even the flowers? How startling
    was the sound
Of pistil! Awed, intent, she caught at clues;
Meticulously quivering at the thought
Of bees; and blushing deeply when he spoke
In baritone of male virtue in the rose.
Through all, the evasive academic phrase,
Putting out vaguely sensitive tentacles
That instantly withdrew from what they
    touched,

[277]

Implied that he could view, quite unper-
    turbed,
All theories, and remain detached, aloft
Among the gods, in philosophic calm;
Nay, by his critical logic was endowed
With something loftier.

              What were gods to him,
Who, being ephemeral, mortal, born to die,
Could, over the port of Corpus and All Souls
Mellowed in classic cellars, quiz the powers
That doomed him, as the aristocrat of thought
Looks through ironical lorgnettes at the might
Of Demos round his tumbril. They lived on,
Wasting their nectar, wrecking worlds on
    worlds.
He had risen, at least, superior to all that.
He held it somewhat barbarous, vulgar, crude
To wallow in such profusion as the gods.
All this implied, not spoken; for he found
His final causes in his dry pressed flowers;
Proved that he knew—none better—all the
    tribe
Who had dragged a net of Latin through the
    fields;

Proved that some flowers, at least, had never
    changed
Through many centuries. The black-seeded
    poppy
Was known to Homer. He rolled out the
    lines.
Almonds, the bitter-kernelled and the sweet,
Were tasted by the prophets; and he found
White-seeded sesamum, in the night of time,
Among the old Egyptians. . . .
He showed that, while his library was vast,
Fragrant with leather, crested, tooled, and
    gilt,
He had closed the Book of Nature, and, on
    the whole,
Despite his open mind, dismissed the views
Of this—er—new philosopher, with a smile
That, don-wise, almost seemed to ask aloud,
"Who is he, after all?" Not one of *us*.
Why weigh his facts, then, further, since we
    hold
The official seals of truth in this our time.
Such men are always wrong. They come and
    go.

THE TORCH-BEARERS

The breeze would soon blow over.

All this implied,
Not spoken, in that small dry steady smile,
Doctor Daubeny gathered up his tails
And made one definite and emphatic point
By sitting down, while some eight hundred
    hands
Acclaimed his perfect don-hood.

Henslow rose,
A little nervously. Had much pleasure,
    though . . .
And turned to Mr. Huxley. Would he
    speak?
A whisper passed, a queer new stillness
    gripped
The expectant crowd. The clock ticked audi-
    bly
Not yet, not yet! A sense of change at
    hand
Stole through the silence, like the first cool
    breath
That, over a great ship's company at night,
Steals through the port-holes from the open
    sea.

[280]

Then, with sure foresight, seeing the clash to
    come,
The strange young man with the determined
    mouth
And quick dark eyes rose grimly, and flung
    down
A single sentence, like a gyve of steel
Wrenched from the wrists to set the strong
    hands free
For whatsoever need might rise, if clock
And *Zeitgeist* changed their quiet *Not Yet* to
    Now.
"A general audience, sir, where sentiment
May interfere, unduly interfere,
With intellect"—as a thin steel wire drawn
    tight
By an iron winch, the hush grew tense and
    rang
Low, hard, clear, cold—*"is not a fitting place*
For this discussion."
                Silence, and the clock,
Two great allies, the surest of them all,
Dead silence, and the voice *Not Yet, Not Yet,*
A cough, the creak of the chair as he sat down,

[281]

A shuffle of feet, the chairman's baffled face,
Then little indignant mutterings round the
hall,
Turning to gasps of mockery. Insolence?—
no,—
Sheer weakness, full retreat!
                              The Bishop raised
His eye-brows, looked at the dense disflat-
tered crowds,
And had no further fear. The battle was
won.
Victory, of the only kind he knew,
Was in his hands. Retreat must now be
turned
Into full rout. He glanced at Owen,—met
His little sardonic smile with a wise nod,
As if to say, "Ah, just as we foresaw."
Excited clerics caught the flying hint
And whispered, eyes agog—"You noticed
that?
He's a great man, the Bishop? What a brow!
And Owen, too. Of course, they know; they
know;
And understand each other, thick as thieves."

Then Owen rose; waved Huxley's empty ex-
　　cuse
Remorselessly aside; and plunged right on,
Declaring there were facts, whereby the
　　crowd
Could very fitly judge.
　　　　　　　　　　The crowd's own feet
Tapped a benign applause.
　　　　　　　　　　Then came the facts,
Facts from a realm that Huxley had made his
　　own.
The brain of the gorilla—some one turned
A faint hysterical laugh into a sneeze—
Linked it more closely to the lowest groups
Of QUADRUMANA.
　　　　　　　　　　"Quadru—what-did-he-say?"
Whispered Miss Pym unconsciously to her-
　　self,
"Mana, four-handed," clerical whiskers
　　breathed,
With Evangelical titillance in her ear,
"Apes, monkeys, all the things that climb up
　　trees.
Says the gorilla's more like them than us."

[283]

"Thank you." Eliza Pym inclined her head
A little stiffly.

             Had the world gone mad?
Was some one in the background trying to find
A pedigree for mankind among the brutes?
Absurd, of course, and yet—one must confess
How like they were in some things.   Unto
    each
A mouth, a nose, two eyes, flesh, blood, and
    bones
Of the same pattern.

             Comic enough, and weird;
But what became of Genesis, then, and God?
If all these whiskered men but one or two
So utterly disbelieved it, why discuss
Degrees of kinship? Surely the gulf was fixed
Wide as the severance between heaven and
    hell.
Then, in one dreadful gleam, she seemed to
    see
The rows of whiskered listeners, darkly
    perched,
Herself among them, on long swaying boughs,
Mesmerised, and all dumbly staring down

THE BOOK OF EARTH

With horrible fascination at great eyes,
Green moons of cruelty, steadily smouldering,
In depths that—smelt of tigers; or the salts
Unstoppered by the vicar's wife in front.

Smile at Eliza Pym with Shadow-of-a-Leaf;
But only if your inward sight can see
Her memories, too—a child's uplifted face,
The clean white cot, the fluttering nursery
 fire;
Old days, old faces, teaching her those lines
From Blake, about a Lamb. Yet that—why
 that
Might be the clue they lacked in all this talk
Of our dumb kinsfolk. If she could but speak
And—hint it! Why don't Bishops think of
 things
Like that, she wondered.
     Owen resumed his chair
With loud applause.
     That grim young man again,
Huxley, was on his feet, his dark eyes lit
With thrice the vital power of all the rest.
In one cool sentence, like a shining lance,

He touched the centre of his opponent's
    shield,
And ended all the shuffling, all the doubts
Of where he stood, how far he dared to go,
If truth required it. He could not accept
Those facts from any authority; gave direct
Unqualified contradiction to those facts;
And pledged himself to justify this course,
Unusual as it seemed perhaps—elsewhere.
"Elsewhere," and as he said it, came a gleam
Into his face, reflected from the heights
Where a tribunal sits whose judgment holds
Not for the fleeting moment, but all time.

"Elsewhere"—the Bishop smiled. He had not
    caught
That gleam. "Elsewhere" was only another
    sign
Of weakness, even timidity perhaps,
And certainly retreat, not from the truth
(He felt so sure of that) but from the might
And deep resources of the established powers
Whose influence ruled the world.
                "Elsewhere" for him

Meant Saturday, and here.   The lists were
    set,
The battle joined, and the great issue plain,—
Whether the human race came straight from
    God,
Or traced its dark descent back to the brute,
And left his creed a wreck of hollow towers,
The haunt of bats and owls.   His time to strike
Would come on Saturday.   Pleadings of "else-
    where"
Would not avail.   He set his jaw.   Please
    God,
He meant to drive this victory crashing home,
And make an end of Darwin once for all.
So closed the first strange scene.
                       The rumour spread
Everywhere, of the Bishop's grim intent.
Saturday's crowd, an hour before its time
Choked all the doors, and crammed the long
    west hall.
Black-coated members of all shades of
    thought,
Knowledge and doubt and bigotry, crushed
    their sides

THE TORCH-BEARERS

In chair-packed rows together (Eliza Pym
Among them, with her startled innocent eyes).
A bevy of undergraduates at the back,
Quietly thoughtful, held their watching brief
For youth and for the future. Fame to come
Already touched the brows of a rare few
With faint leaf-shadows of her invisible
    wreath:
Green, the philosopher, gazing at the world
With youth's aloofness, and that inward light
Which shines from Oxford still; not far away
The young historian of the coloured stream
Of outward life, the ancestral pageantry
Of England, and its tributary rills
Flowing in dawn-gleams out of the mists of
    time.
There, too, in front, with atavistic face
And Vandyke beard, so oddly like the king
Who loved Nell Gwynne, sat Admiral Fitz-
    Roy,
Late captain of the *Beagle,* quite prick-eared
With personal curiosity. Twice he told
His neighbour that, by George, he wouldn't
    ha' missed

THE BOOK OF EARTH

This Donnybrook Fair for anything. He had
    sailed
With Darwin round the world. They used to
    call him
The old philosopher. Heard the bosun once,
Pointing the officers out—damned funny it
    was!—
"That's Captain FitzRoy. That's the second
    mate;
And *that*"—pointing a thumb at Darwin's
    back—
"*That's* our Fly-Catcher!"
                        Best of fellows, too,
But queer. He'd tell you, in the simplest
    way
—As if it meant no more than pass the salt,—
Something that knocked you endways; calmly
    shift
.A mountain-range, in half a dozen words,
And sink it in the sea.
                    In fact, FitzRoy
Felt it his duty more than once, by George,
To expostulate; told him plainly he'd upset
Genesis and the Church; and then there'd be

The devil and all to pay. And now, by
    George,
He'd done it; and her Majesty's Admiral
Had come on purpose, all the way from town,
To hear and see the end of it.

                       So he said,
Not wholly understanding why he came,—
The memory of a figure rapt and bowed
Over a shell, or finding in the rocks,
As though by wizardry, relics of lost worlds;
Moments that, by a hardly noticed phrase,
Had touched with orderly meaning and new
    light
The giant flaws and foldings in the hills;
Moments when, in the cabin, he had stared
Into the "old philosopher's" microscope,
And seen the invisible speck in a water-
    drop
Grow to a great rose-window of radiant life
In an immense cathedral.

                  Vaguely enough,
Perhaps in the dimmest hinterland of his
    mind,
There lurked a quiet suspicion that, after all,

His queer old friend *had* hit on something
    queer.
Three places off, his face a twinkling mask
Of keen Scots humour, Robert Chambers
    glanced
Quietly at his watch, to hide a smile
When some one who had "written the Ves-
    tiges,"
And only half denied it, met his eye.

The vacant platform glared expectancy,
And held the gaze now of the impatient
    crowd.

Then Henslow led the conquering Bishop in.
Two rows of clerics, halfway down the hall,
Drummed for their doughty champion with
    their heels.
Above, in each recessed high window-seat,
Bishop-adoring ladies clapped their hands.

The rest filed in, mere adjuncts, modest foils.
Hooker and Lubbock and Huxley took their
    chairs

THE TORCH-BEARERS

On Henslow's left. The beautiful gaitered
    legs,
By their divine prerogative, on his right,
So carelessly crossed, more eloquently than
    words
Assured the world that everything was well,
And their translation into forms of speech
A mere formality. Next to the Bishop sat
A Transatlantic visitor with a twang,
One Doctor Draper, his hard wrinkled skin
Tinged by the infinite coffee he absorbed,
A gaunt bone-coloured desert, unassuaged.
He was a grim diplomatist, as befits
A pilgrim of the cosmos; ready at Rome
To tickle the Romans; and, if bishops ruled,
And found themselves at odds with freeborn
    souls
Outside the Land of Freedom, he'd befriend
Bishops, bring in the New World, stars and
    all,
To rectify that balance, and take home
For souvenir, with a chip of the pyramids,
The last odd homages of the obsequious
    Old.

The president called him for his opening
    speech.
He stood and beamed, enjoying to the full
The sense that, with his mighty manuscript,
He could delay the antagonists for an hour.
He cleared his throat. He took from a little
    box
A small black lozenge; popped it into his
    mouth,
Leisurely rolled it under a ruminant tongue,
Then placidly drawled his most momentous
    words:
"Proh-fessur Henslow, Bishop Wilbur-force,
Members, AND *friends, in this historic hall,*
I assk first, AIR *we a fortooitous*
Con-course of atoms?" Half unconsciously,
He struck at once to the single central heart
Of all the questions asked by every age;
As though he saw what only Shadow-of-a-
    Leaf
Had watched last night, as in a crystal
    globe,
That scene preparing, the interweaving clues
Whose inconceivable intricacy at length,

[293]

By "chance," as blind men call it, through the
    maze
Of life and time, at the one right juncture
    brought
Two shadows, face to face, in an Oxford
    Street,
Chambers and Huxley. "You'll be there to-
    morrow."—
"No, I leave Oxford now."—

                       "The enemy means
To annihilate Darwin. You will not desert
    us?"—
"If you say that, I stay."

                     Each to his place
Had moved in his own orbit, like a star,
Or like an atom, free-will at one with law,
In the unplanned plan of the Master-Drama-
    tist,
Where Doctor Draper blindly played his
    part
And asked his pregnant question. He droned
    on,
For one enormous hour, starkly maintained
That Europe, in its intellectual life,

By mere "fortooity," never could have flow-
    ered
To such results as blushed before him there
In that historic hall of halls to-night.
If Darwin thought so, he took leave to stand
Beside them, and to smile the vast calm smile
Of Arizona's desert distances,
Till all such dragon thoughts had coiled
    away.
He took his chair. The great debate began.
For prelude came a menacing growl of storm.
A furious figure rose, like a sperm-whale,
Out of the seething audience. A huge man,
With small, hot, wicked eyes and cavernous
    mouth,
Bellowed his own ferocious claim to speak
On economic grounds. He had subscribed
His guineas, ringing guineas of red gold,
Ungrudgingly for years; but prophesied
Withdrawal of all such guineas, on all sides,
From this Association, if it failed
To brand these most abominable views
As blasphemous, bearing on their devilish
    brows,

Between their horns, the birth-mark of the
    Beast.
This last word hissed, he sank again. At once,
Ere Henslow found his feet or spoke a word,
Up leapt a raw-boned parson from the North,
To seize his moment's fame. With sawing
    arm
The Reverend Dingle, like a windmill, vowed
He'd prove upon the blackboard, in white
    chalk,
By diagram—and the chalk was in his hand—
"That mawnkey and mahn had separate pedi-
    grees.
Let A here be the mawnkey, and B the mahn."
Loud laughter; shouts of "mawnkey!" and
    "sit down"
Extinguished him. He sat; and Henslow
    quelled
The hubbub with one clarion-clear demand,
Dictated, surely, by the ironic powers
Who had primed the Bishop and prepared his
    fall:
"Gentlemen, this discussion now must rest
On scientific grounds."

THE BOOK OF EARTH

                              At once there came
Calls for the Bishop, who, rising from his
    chair,
Urged by the same invisible ironies,
Remarked that his old friend, Professor
    Beale,
Had something to say *first*. That weighty
    first
Conveyed the weight of his own words to
    come.
Urged still by those invisible ones, his friend
Dug the pit deeper; modestly declared,
Despite his keen worn face and shoulders
    bowed
In histologic vigils, that he felt
His knowledge quite inadequate; and the way
Was made straight—for the Bishop.
The Bishop rose, mellifluous, bland, adroit.

A gesture, lacking only the lawn sleeves
To make it perfect, delicately conveyed
His comfortable thought—that what amazed
The sheepfold must be folly.
                              Half the throng,

His own experience told him, had not grasped
The world-inweaving argument, could not
    think
In æons. Æons, then, would be dismissed
As vague and airy fantasies. He might choose
His facts at will, unchallenged. He stood
    there
Secure that his traditions could not fail,
Basing his faith on schemes of thought de-
    signed
By authorised "thinkers" in pure artistry,
As free from Nature's law as coloured blocks
That children play with on the nursery
    hearth,
And puzzle about and shift and twist and turn
Until the beautiful picture, as ordained,
Comes out, exact to the pattern, and reveals
The artificer's plan, the pattern, as arranged,
By bishops, politic statesmen, teachers, guides,
Who hold it in reserve, their final test
Of truth, for times like this. He had been so
    sure
Of something deeper than all schemes of
    thought

THE BOOK OF EARTH

That he had all too lightly primed himself
With "facts" to match their fables; hastily
     crammed
Into his mind's convenient travelling bag
(Sound leather, British) all that he re-
     quired,—
Not truth, but "a good argument." He had
     asked
Owen, who hated Huxley, to provide it;
And he had brought it with him,—not the
     truth,
Not even facts, those unrelated crumbs
Of truth, the abiding consecrated whole.
He had brought his borrowed "facts," misun-
     derstood,
To meet, for the first time in all his life,
Stark earnest thought, wrestling for truth
     alone,
As men on earth discerned it. He had prayed,
With something deeper than blind make-be-
     lieve,
Thy will be done on earth; and yet, and yet,
The law wherein that will might be discerned,
The law wherein that unity of heaven

[299]

And earth might yet be found (could he but
    trust
The truth, could he believe that his own God
Lived in the living truth), he waved aside.
These others had not found it, but they kept
One faith that he had lost. Though it should
    slay them,
They trusted in the truth. They could not see
Where it might lead them. Only at times they
    felt
As they deciphered the dark Book of Earth
That, following its majestic rhythm of law,
They followed the true path, the eternal way
Of That which reigns. Prophetic flashes
    came.
Words that the priest mechanically intoned
Burned upon Huxley's keen ironical page
Like sudden sapphires, drawing their deeper
    light
From that celestial City which endures
Because it hath foundations: *Shall I come*
Before the Eternal with burnt offerings?
Hath not the Eternal showed thee what is
    good,

That thou do justly and mercifully, and walk
Humbly with the Eternal?

O, irony of the Master-dramatist,
Who set once more those lists; and sent His
        truth
Unrecognised, as of old, to fight for life
And prove itself in struggle and raise once
        more
A nobler world above the world out-worn,
Crushing all easy sophistry, though it stood
Garbed as the priest of God.
                            The Bishop seized
His diplomatic vantage. The blunt truth
Of Huxley's warning offered itself to him
As a rash gambit in their game of—tact.
He seized it; gracefully smoothed the ruffled
        pride
Of that great audience, trained in a sound
        school
To judge by common-sense.
                            His mobile face
Revealed much that his politic words con-
        cealed.

[301]

THE TORCH-BEARERS

His strength was in that sound old British
way—
Derision of all things that transcend its codes
In life, thought, art; the moon-calf's happy
creed
That, if a moon-calf only sees the moon
In thoughts that range the cosmos, his broad
grin
Sums the whole question; there's no more to
see.
In all these aids, an innocent infidel,
The Bishop put his trust; and, more than all,
In vanity, the vacant self-conceit
That, when it meets the masters of the mind
And finds them bowed before the Inscrutable
Power,
Accepts their reverence and humility
As tribute, due acknowledgment of fool's
right
To give the final judgment, and annul
The labour of a life-time in an hour.
Dulcetly, first, he scoffed at Darwin's facts.
"Rock-pigeons now were what they had al-
ways been.

THE BOOK OF EARTH

Species had never changed. What were the
    proofs
Even of the variation they required
To make this theory possible? We had heard
Mysterious rumours of a long-legged sheep
Somewhere in Yorkshire (laughter). Let me
    ask
Professor Huxley, here upon the left
(All eyes on Huxley), who believes himself
Descended from an ape (chuckles of glee),
How recently this happened."
                  The Bishop turned,
All smiling insolence, "May I beg to know
If this descent is on your father's side,
Or on your mother's?"
                He paused, to let the crowd
Bellow its laughter. The unseen ironies
Had trapped him and his flock; and neither
    knew.
But Huxley knew. He turned, with a grim
    smile,
And while the opposing triumph rocked and
    pealed,
Struck one decisive palm upon his knee,

[303]

THE TORCH-BEARERS

And muttered low—"*The Lord hath delivered him
Into my hands.*"

His neighbour stared and thought
His wits were wandering. Yet that undertone
Sounded more deadly, had more victory in it,
Than all the loud-mouthed minute's dying
roar.

It died to a tense hush. The Bishop closed
In solemn diapason. Darwin's views
Degraded woman. They debased mankind,
And contradicted God's most Holy Word.
Applause! Applause! The hall a quivering
mist
Of clapping hands. From every windowseat
A flutter of ladies' handkerchiefs and shrill
cries
As of white swarming sea-gulls. The black
rows
Of clerics all exchanging red-faced nods,
And drumming with their feet, as though to
fill
A hundred-pedalled organ with fresh wind.

THE BOOK OF EARTH

The Bishop, like a *Gloire de Dijon* rose
With many-petalled smiles, his plump right
    hand
Clasped in a firm congratulatory grip
Of hickory-bones by Draper of New York;
Who had small faith in what the Bishop said
But heard the cheers, and gripped him as a
    man
Who never means to let this good thing go.
Motionless, on the left, the observant few,
The silent delegates of a sterner power,
With grave set faces, quietly looking on.
At last the tumult, as all tumult must,
Sank back to that deep silence. Henslow
    turned
To Huxley without speaking. Once again
The clock ticked audibly, but its old "Not
    Yet"
Had somehow, in that uproar, in the face
Of that tumultuous mockery, changed to
    Now!

The lean tall figure of Huxley quietly rose.
He looked for a moment thoughtfully at the
    crowd;

Saw rows of hostile faces; caught the grin
Of ignorant curiosity; here and there,
A hopeful gleam of friendship; and, far back,
The young, swift-footed, waiting for the fire.
He fixed his eyes on these—then, in low tones,
Clear, cool, incisive, *"I have come here,"* he
    said,
"In the cause of Science only."
                  He paused again.
Then, striking the mockery out of the mock-
    er's face,
His voice rang out like steel—
              "I have heard nothing
To prejudice the case of my august
Client, who, as I told you, is not here."
At once a threefold picture flashed upon me,
A glimpse, far off, through eyes of Shadow-
    of-a-Leaf,
First, of a human seeker, there at Down,
Gathering his endless cloud of witnesses
From rocks, from stones, from trees; and from
    the signs
In man's own body of life's æonian way;
But, far above him, clothed with purer light,

THE BOOK OF EARTH

The stern, majestic Spirit of living Truth;
And, more august than even his prophets
    knew,
Through that eternal Spirit, the primal
    Power
Returning into a world of faiths out-worn.

Once more, as he spoke on, a thousand years
Were but as yesterday. If these truths were
    true,
This theory flooded the whole world with
    light.
Could we believe that the Creator set
In mockery all these birth-signs in the world,
Or once in a million years had wrecked His
    work
'And shaped, in a flash, a myriad lives anew,
Bearing in their own bodies all the signs
Of their descent from those that He de-
    stroyed?
Who left that ancient leaf within the flower?
Who hid within the reptile those lost fins,
And under the skin of the sea-floundering
    whale

THE TORCH-BEARERS

The bones of the lost thigh?   Who dusked the
     foal
With shadowy stripes, and under its hoof con-
     cealed
Those ancient birdlike feet of its lost kin?
Who matched that hoof with a rosy finger-
     nail,
Or furled that point within the human ear?
Who had imprinted in the body of man,
And in his embryo, all those intricate signs
Of his forgotten lineage, even those gills
Through which he drew his breath once in the
     sea?

The speaker glanced at his antagonist.
"You think all this too marvellous to be true;
Yet you believe in miracles.   You think
The unfolding of this complicated life
Around us, out of a simple primal form,
Impossible; yet you know that every man
Before his birth, a few brief years ago,
Was once no more than a single living cell.
You think it ends your theory of creation.
You say that God made *you;* and yet you know

—And reconcile your creed with what you
    know—
That you yourself originally"—he held up
A gleaming pencil-case—"were a little piece
Of matter, not so large as the end of this.
                But if you ask, in fine,
Whether I'd be ashamed to claim descent
From that poor animal with the stooping gait
And low intelligence, who can only grin
And chatter as we pass by, or from a *man*
Who could use high position and great gifts
To crush one humble seeker after truth—
I hesitate, but"—an outburst of applause
From all who understood him drowned the
    words.
He paused. The clock ticked audibly again.
Then, quietly measuring every word, he drove
The sentence home. "I asserted and repeat
A man would have no cause to feel ashamed
Of being descended through vast tracts of
    time
From that poor ape.
              Were there an ancestor
Whom I could not recall without a sense

Of shame, it were a *man,* so placed, so gifted,
Who sought to sway his hearers from the truth
By aimless eloquence and by skilled appeals
To their religious prejudice."

                      Was it the truth
That conquered, or the blind sense of the blow
Justly considered, delivered, and driven
    home,
That brought a crash of applause from half
    the house?
And more (for even the outright enemy
Joined in that hubbub), though indignant
    cries,
Protested vainly, "Abominable to treat
The Bishop so!"

              The Bishop sat there dumb.
Eliza Pym, adding her own quaint touch
Of comedy, saw that pencil shine again
In Huxley's hand; compared it, at a glance
Of fawn-like eyes, with the portentous form
In gaiters; felt the whole world growing
    strange;
Drew one hysterical breath, and swooned
    away.

V

THE *VERA CAUSA*

AND yet, and yet, the victor knew too well
His victory had a relish of the dust.
Even while the plaudits echoed in his ears,
It troubled him. When he pondered it that
      night,
A finer shame had touched him. He had used
The weapons of his enemy at the last;
And, if he had struck his enemy down for
      truth,
He had struck him down with weapons he de-
      spised.
He had used them with a swifter hand and
      eye,
A subtler cunning; and he had set his heel
On those who took too simply to their hearts
A tale, whose ancient imagery enshrined
A mystery that endured. He had proclaimed
A fragment of a truth which, he knew well,

Left the true Cause in darkness. Did he
    know
More of that Cause than *Genesis?* Could he
    see
Farther into that darkness than the child
Folding its hands in prayer?

                More clearly far
Than Darwin, whom he had warned of it, he
    knew
The bounds of this new law; bade him be-
    ware
Of his repeated dogma—*Nature makes*
No leap. He pointed always to the Abyss
Of darkness round the flickering spark of light
Upheld by Science. Had Wilberforce been
    armed
With knowledge and the spiritual steel
Of Saint Augustine, who had also seen,
Even in his age, a ladder of life to heaven,
There had been a victory of another kind
To lighten through the world.

             And Darwin knew it;
But, while he marshalled his unnumbered
    truths,

He lost the Truth; as one who takes com-
    mand
Of multitudinous armies in the night,
And strives to envisage, in one sweep of the
    mind,
Each squadron and each regiment of the
    whole,
Ever the host that swept through his mind's
    eye,
Though all in ordered ranks and files, ob-
    scured
Army on army the infinite truth beyond.
The gates of Beauty closed against his mind,
And barred him out from that eternal realm,
Whose lucid harmonies on our night bestow
Glimpses of absolute knowledge from above;
Unravelling and ennobling, making clear
Much that had baffled us, much that else was
    dark;
So that the laws of Nature shine like roads,
Firm roads that lead through a significant
    world
Not downward, from the greater to the less,
But up to the consummate soul of all.

He could not follow them now. Back, back
    and back,
He groped along the dark diminishing road.
The ecstasy of music died away.
The poet's vision melted into a dream.
He knew his loss, and mourned it; but it
    marred
Not only his own happiness, as he thought.
It blurred his vision, even of his own truths.

He looked long at the butterfly's radiant
    wings,
Pondered their blaze of colour, and believed
That butterfly wooers choosing their bright
    mates
Through centuries of attraction and desire
Evolved this loveliness. For he only saw
The blaze of colour, the flash that lured the
    eye.
He did not see the exquisite pattern there,
The diamonded fans of the under-wing,
Inlaid with intricate harmonies of design;
The delicate little octagons of pearl,
The moons like infinitesimal fairy flowers,

THE BOOK OF EARTH

The lozenges of gold, and grey, and blue
All ordered in an intellectual scheme,
Where form to form responded and faint
    lights
Echoed faint lights, and shadowy fringes ran
Like Elfin curtains on a silvery thread,
Shadow replying to shadow through the
    whole.

Did eyes of the butterfly wooer mark all
    this,—
A subtlety too fine for half mankind?
He tossed a shred of paper on to his lawn;
He saw the white wings blindly fluttering
    round it.
He did not hear the whisper of Shadow-of-a-
    Leaf,
Was this their exquisite artistry of choice?
Had wooers like these evolved this loveliness?

He groped into the orchestral universe
As one who strives to trace a symphony
Back to its cause, and with laborious care
Feels with his hand the wood of the violins,

And bids you mark—O good, bleak, honest
    soul,
So fearful of false hopes!—that all is hollow.
He tells you on what tree the wood was
    grown.
He plucks the catgut, tells you whence it
    came,
Gives you the name and pedigree of the cat;
Nay, even affirms a mystery, and will talk
Of sundry dark vibrations that affect
The fleshly instrument of the human ear;
And so, with a world-excluding accuracy—
O, never doubt that every step was true!—
Melts the great music into less than air
And misses everything.
               Everything! On one side
The music soaring endlessly through heavens
Within the human soul; on the other side,
The unseen Composed of whose transcendent
    life
The music speaks in souls made still to hear.
He clung to his *vera causa*. In that law
He saw the way of the Power, but not the
    Power

Determining the way.   Did men reject
The laws of Newton, binding all the worlds,
Because they still knew nothing of the Power
That bound them?   The stone fell.   He knew
    not why.
The sun controlled the planets, and the law
Was constant; but the mystery of it was
    masked
Under a name; and no man knew the Power
That gripped the worlds in that unchanging
    bond,
Or whether, in the twinkling of an eye,
The Power might not release them from that
    bond,
As a hand opens, and the wide universe
Change in a flash, and vanish like a shadow,
As prophets had foretold.
                   He could not think
That chance decreed the boundless march of
    law
He saw in the starry heavens.   Yet he could
    think
Of "chance" on earth; and, while he thought,
    declare

"Chance" was not "chance" but law unrecog-
        nised;
Then, even while he said it, he would use
The ambiguous word, base his own law on
        "chance";
And, even while he used it, there would move
Before his eyes in every flake of colour,
Inlaid upon the butterfly's patterned wing,
Legions of atoms wheeling each to its place
In ever constant law; and he knew well
That, even in the living eye that saw them,
The self-same Power that bound the starry
        worlds
Controlled a myriad atoms, every one
An ordered system; and in every cloud
Of wind-blown dust and every breaking
        wave
Upon the storm-tossed sea, an infinite host
Of infinitesimal systems moved by law
Each to its place; and, in each growing flower,
Myriads of atoms like concentred suns
And planets, these to the leaf and those to the
        crown,
Moved in unerring order, and by a law

That bound all heights and depths of the uni-
    verse,
In an unbroken unity. By what Power?
There was one Power, one only known to man,
That could determine action. Herschel knew
    it;
The power whereby the mind uplifts the hand
And lets it fall, the living personal Will.

Ah, but his task, his endless task on earth,
Bent his head earthward. He must find the
    way
Before he claimed the heights. No Newton
    he;
Though men began to acclaim him and his
    law
As though they solved all mysteries and an-
    nulled
All former creeds, and changed the heart of
    heaven.
No Newton he; not even a Galileo;
But one who patiently, doggedly laboured on,
As Tycho Brahe laboured in old days,
Numbering the stars, recording fact on fact,

THE TORCH-BEARERS

For those, who, after centuries, might dis-
    cern
The meaning and the cause of what he saw.
Visions of God and Heaven were not for
    him,
Unless his "facts" revealed them, as the crown
Of his own fight for knowledge.

                              It might be
The final test of man, the narrow way
Proving him worthy of immortal life,
That he should face this darkness and this
    death
Worthily and renounce all easy hope,
All consolation, all but the wintry smile
Upon the face of Truth as he discerns it,
Here upon earth, his only glimmer of light,
Leading him onward to an end unknown.
Faith! Faith! O patient, inarticulate soul,
If this were faithlessness, there was a Power,
So whispered Shadow-of-a-Leaf, that shared
    it with him;
The Power that bowed His glory into dark-
    ness
To make a world in suffering and in death,

THE BOOK OF EARTH

The passionate price that even the Omnipo-
  tent
Must pay for love, and love's undying crown.

He hardly heard the whisper; could not hear
  it
And keep his own resolve. He bowed his
  head
In darkness; and, henceforth, those inward
  gates
Into the realms of the supernal light
Began to close.
            He knew that they were closing;
And yet—was this the dark key to Crea-
  tion?—
He shared the ecstasy also; shared that sense
Of triumph; broke the Bread and drank the
  Wine
In sacred drops and morsels of the truth;
Shared, in renouncement of all else but
  truth,
A sense that he could never breathe in words
To any one else, a sense that in this age
It was expedient that a man should lose

The glory, and die this darker new-found
    death,
To save the people from their rounded creeds,
Their faithless faith, and crowns too lightly
    won.

      *   *   *   *   *   *   *

O, yet the memory of one midnight hour!
*Would that she knew. Would God that she
    knew now* . . .
Truer than all his knowledge was that cry;
The cry of the blind life struggling through
    the dark,
Upward . . . the blind brow lifted to the un-
    seen.

He groped along the dark unending way
And saw, although he knew not what he saw,
Out of the struggle of life, a mightier law
Emerging; and, when man could rise no
    higher
By the fierce law of Nature, he beheld
Nature herself at war against herself.
He heard, although he knew not what he
    heard,

A Voice that, triumphing over her clashing
chords,
Resolved them into an infinite harmony.
Whose was that Voice? What Power within the flesh
Cast off the flesh for a glory in the mind,
And leapt to victory in self-conquering love?
What Voice, whose Power, cast Nature underfoot
In Bruno, when the flames gnawed at his
flesh;
In Socrates; and, in those obscure Christs
Who daily die; and, though none other sees,
Lay hands upon the wheel of the universe
And master it; and the sun stands dark at
noon?
These things he saw but dimly. All his life
He moved along the steep and difficult way
Of Truth in darkness; but the Voice of Truth
Whispered in darkness, out of the mire and
clay,
And through the blood-stained agony of the
world,
"Fear nothing. Follow Me. I *am* the Way."

So, when Death touched him also, and Eng-
    land bore
His dust into her deepening innermost shrine,
The Voice he heard long since, and could not
    hear,
Rose like the fuller knowledge, given by
    Death
To one that could best lead him upward now,
Rose like a child's voice, opening up the
    heavens,
I am the Resurrection and the Life.

X—EPILOGUE

UP the Grand Canyon the full morning
   flowed.
I heard the voices moving through the
   abyss
With the deep sound of pine-woods, league on
   league
Of singing boughs, each separate, each a
   voice,
Yet all one music;
                    The Eternal Mind
Enfolds all changes, and can never change.

Man is not exiled from this Majesty,
The inscrutable Reality, which he shares
In his immortal essence. Man that doubts
All but the sensuous veils of colour and sound,
The appearances that he can measure and
   weigh,
Trusts, as the very fashioner of his doubt,

[325]

THE TORCH-BEARERS

*The imponderable thought that weighs the
worlds,
The invisible thought that sees; thought that
reveals
The miracle of the eternal paradox—
The pure unsearchable Being that cannot be
Yet* IS, *and still creates and governs all;
A Power that, being unknowable, is best
known;
For this transcendent Being can reply
To every agony, "I am that which waits
Beyond the last horizon of your pain,
Beyond your wildest hope, your last despair,
Above your heaven, and deeper than your
hell.
There is not room on earth for what ye seek.
Is there not room in Me?"*

       *Time is a shadow
Of man's own thought. Things past and
things to come
Are closed in that full circle. He lives and
reigns;
Dies with the dying bird; and, in its death
Receives it to His heart. No leaf can fall*

THE BOOK OF EARTH

Without Him; who, for ever pouring out
His passion into worlds that shall attain
Love in the highest at last, returns for ever
Along these roads of suffering and of death,
With all their lives upgathered to His heart
Into the heaven of heavens.   How else could
      life
Lay hold on its infinitude, or win
The strength to walk with Love in complete
      light?
For, as a child that learns to walk on earth,
Life learns these little rhythms of earthly law,
Listens to simple seas that ebb and flow,
And spells the large bright order of the stars
Wherein the moving Reason is revealed
To man's up-struggling mind, or breathed like
      song
Into the quiet heart, as love to love.
So, step by step, the spirit of man ascends
Through joy and grief; and is withdrawn by
      death
From the sweet dust that might content it here
Into His kingdom, the one central goal
Of the universal agony.   He lives.

THE TORCH-BEARERS

He lives and reigns, throned above Space and
    Time;
And, in that realm, freedom and law are one;
Fore-knowledge and all-knowledge and free-
    will,
Make everlasting music.
                     Far away
Along the unfathomable abyss it flowed,
A harmony so consummate that it shared
The silence of the sky; a song so deep
That only the still soul could hear it now:
New every morning the creative Word
Moves upon chaos. Yea, our God grows
    young.
Here, now, the eternal miracle is renewed
Now, and for ever, God makes heaven and
    earth.